Solo Practice Guidebook

THE AMERICAN ASSOCIATION
OF NURSE ATTORNEYS

DISCLOSURE

AUTHORS HAVE NO FINANCIAL INTERESTS OR RELATIONSHIPS WITH ANY OF THE PRODUCTS OR PROGRAMS SUGGESTED IN THIS GUIDEBOOK, NOR DO THEY ENDORSE THEM.

DISCLAIMER

WHILE THIS GUIDEBOOK OFFERS GUIDANCE ON SOLO PRACTICE, IT SHOULD NOT BE CONSTRUED AS LEGAL ADVICE.

IBSN number:
979-8-218-75788-5 (hardback)
978-1-7359347-9-2 (paperback)

THE AMERICAN ASSOCIATION OF NURSE ATTORNEYS FOUNDATION

The American Association of Nurse Attorneys (TAANA) Foundation was incorporated in 1984 as a Maryland charitable organization by Cynthia Ellen Northrop, the first nurse attorney and visionary leader behind its formation. Several TAANA members, including myself, knew Cynthia Northrop and were professionally influenced by her.

The Foundation's purpose is to operate exclusively for charitable or educational purposes and provide financial support to recognized charitable institutions or to further charitable or academic works. The TAANA Foundation fosters the education of nurse attorneys, impacts health policy and law by honoring leaders, and supports issues important to the professional organization. The Foundation is an avenue to help nurse attorneys give back to their communities.

Some of the Foundation's accomplishments are:

- Establishment of an academic scholarship, in perpetuity, in memory of TAANA's founder, Cynthia Northrop. ***The Cynthia Northrop Memorial Scholarship Endowment for Ph.D. Students*** is awarded at the University of Maryland School of Nursing, where Cynthia was a professor. The first scholarship was awarded in 2021.
- Publication of the revised ***Model Curriculum of Legal Content in Nursing Education***.

- Support the ***TAANA Archives*** housed at the library of Boston College, Massachusetts.
- Develop scholarly publications that analyze developments and trends in healthcare law, such as Amicus Briefs, Position Papers, and White Papers, through the ***TAANA Virtual Store.***
- Developed and produced the DVD ***Think Before You Speak*** to prepare nurses for deposition.
- Award ***Student scholarships*** to law school students or first-year nurse attorneys to attend the TAANA annual educational conference.
- Establishment of the ***Mary Eleanor McGarvah*** **Award to honor** Ms. McGarvah's significant contributions to society through humanitarian efforts and the development of public health, law, nursing, and public policy.
- Provide an annual ***Community Grant*** to an organization that provides legal and/or healthcare services to a vulnerable population within the locale of the annual conference.

Contributions fund the Foundation. The TAANA Foundation is a 501(c)3 nonprofit charity. Donations are tax-deductible to the extent of the law. Donations may be made to the Student Scholarship, the general Foundation charitable fund, or in honor or in memory of someone at any time. Donations can be made at the Foundation website, http://www.taana.org/foundation/donation/, by downloading the "printable donation form" on the same page, or with annual membership dues, with registration for TAANA's annual educational conference, contacting the Foundation's Administrator, or in person at the Annual Meeting.

Randi Kopf, RN, MS, JD
President, TAANA Foundation

Table of Contents

Prologue

"Come to the edge," he said.

"We can't, we're afraid!" they responded.

"Come to the edge," he said.

"We can't, we will fall!" they responded.

"Come to the edge," he said.

And so they came.

And he pushed them.

And they flew.

Guillaume Apollinaire

Preface

Welcome to solo practice! The American Association of Nurse Attorneys (TAANA), through the Solo Practice Section, has created this guidebook to assist members who wish to explore solo practice. Whether your background is in larger firm practice or as an organizational employee, the move to solo practice can be daunting. Many of us made this transition without the benefit of the guidance and resources this guidebook hopes to provide.

The Solo Practice Section was created to address the particular needs and interests of the many TAANA members who have chosen an autonomous solo practice. The committee members have a wide range of experience in establishing and running their own businesses and have collaborated to create this guidebook. We have included common issues and foundational information that would have been helpful to us when starting, as well as lessons we have learned along the way. We offer our collective experience in hopes that encouragement and support will make your path easier and more rewarding.

Most of us were challenged by having no background in business or finance. We were nurses. We were lawyers. We were professionals, but we were not accountants, marketers, business operators, or entrepreneurs. We had to acquire those skills to open and run a solo practice. We had to learn how to run a business. This is very challenging. It requires study, reflection, and work. It requires paradigm shifts and uncertainty. But isn't that what we have always done? Haven't nurse attorneys always opened themselves to new challenges and been willing to be inexperienced at something for a while? We are industrious. We are resourceful. We forgo short-term comfort to achieve long-term goals.

Few, if any of us, who have been in solo practice, would return to firm or employee life. It is the best decision we have ever made. It can be yours as well. Why have so many of us chosen to practice law without the structural support of a larger organization? Probably for the same reason you are reading this guidebook. We want flexibility, control, work/life balance, autonomy, and authority that cannot be provided any other way. We want to represent our clients to the best of our ability without being micromanaged. We want to spend as much time as we need on a client's case without being questioned about it. We want to generate income without a firm's billable hour obsession. We want to choose which clients we will represent and which ones we will not. We want to control our schedules. We want to be collegial more than competitive. We want something that is ours. This is why we practice solo. We find it more rewarding, more satisfying, more interesting. We have found that the rewards of embracing the challenges of solo practice are worth it.

We hope this guidebook will provide a blueprint for your journey. It is not intended to provide legal advice, as individual state requirements vary considerably. It is, however, intended to outline the steps you will need to take and our suggestions for taking them.

American naturalist John Burroughs said, "Leap and the net will appear." Here is the net. Leap.

Edie Brous

Solo Practice Section Chair 2021

Introduction

Solo practice is unlike legal work in a firm or other organization. The safety net provided by an organization is no longer there. A managing partner will not be assigning cases, performing conflicts checks, or monitoring your practice. You will manage yourself. Human resources will not remind you of continuing education requirements or other bar association mandates. You will be human resources. There is no colleague in the next room you can question about the ethics of a situation. You will be your own ethics advisor. Full responsibility for knowing the rules in your state will rest on your shoulders.

Those of us participating in the Solo Practice Section of TAANA have weighed the advantages and disadvantages of practicing alone vs. being a firm member or an employee. We decided that the advantages and benefits outweigh the disadvantages and risks.

If you make the same decision, some of the challenges you may face include:

Required Practice Skills	**Solo Practice**	**Firm/Employee**	**Discussed in:**
Business structure/ tax management	You decide your business model, tax management, and staffing choices	Decided by someone else	Chapter 1
Risk management, Liability insurance	Your responsibility	Responsibility assumed by the firm/organization	Chapter 1
Opening a business	Your responsibility	Done for you	Chapter 2

Required Practice Skills	Solo Practice	Firm/Employee	Discussed in:
Financial management	Do it yourself or hire someone under your supervision	Done for you	Chapter 2
Marketing	Do it yourself or hire someone under your supervision	Provided for you	Chapter 3
Scope of practice	Your responsibility	Managed by someone else	Chapter 4
Client selection	YOU ALONE	Selected for you	Chapter 4 Chapter 7
Billing/record-keeping	Do it yourself or hire someone under your supervision	Done for you	Chapter 5
Office management	Do it yourself or hire someone under your supervision	Done for you	Chapter 6
Health insurance/ retirement planning	Provide for yourself and any staff you hire	Provided for you	Chapter 6
Client management	YOU ALONE	Managed by someone else	Chapter 7
Practice specialty	Your choice	Chosen for your	Chapter 8
Your mental and physical health	A self-care priority on your time and schedule	No time allotted; not an expectation	Chapter 9

In this guidebook, we will share our experiences on this journey and provide various tools to help you anticipate and solve problems. Sample practice guides will provide starting points and references as you incorporate these responsibilities into your new solo practice.

There are many career opportunities for nurse attorneys who want to practice as solos. Chapter 8 discusses several areas of law in which our current members practice, with specific considerations for each.

The guidebook has been structured to provide information on the transition—things you must consider and suggestions before getting started. You will be responsible for your own practice and for knowing and remaining compliant with your state bar association requirements. You will be responsible for monitoring changes in ethics rules, continuing legal education (CLE) requirements, tax liabilities, tax payments, pro-bono requirements, and evolving standards of practice. It is a new way of managing your practice.

Solos need to adjust to collegial isolation that is not experienced in other settings. Solo practice allows you to control your schedule, but a work/life balance is sometimes challenging to maintain. Chapter 9 discusses self-care, which is critical to solos.

We are solos, but we have each other. We learn from each other. We grow professionally from our relationships. We support each other. We invite you to join us.

CHAPTER 1

Forming Your Business

Randi Kopf, RN, MS, JD

DISCLOSURE

THE AUTHOR HAS NO FINANCIAL INTERESTS OR RELATIONSHIPS WITH ANY OF THE PRODUCTS OR PROGRAMS SUGGESTED IN THIS CHAPTER, NOR DO THEY ENDORSE THEM.

DISCLAIMER

WHILE THIS CHAPTER GUIDEBOOK OFFERS GUIDANCE ON SOLO PRACTICE, IT SHOULD NOT BE CONSTRUED AS LEGAL ADVICE.

WHERE TO BEGIN

When starting your solo practice, some questions and factors to consider include:

- Why do you want to form a solo law practice?
- What are your personal, professional, and financial goals?
- What type of law do you want to practice?
- How much time do you have to commit to your solo law practice?
    - Consider personal and family commitments
- Where do you want to practice?
- Private office space
    - Shared space with other non-affiliated lawyers
    - Home office
    - Executive services suite
    - Virtual practice—anywhere you are.

THE NAME OF YOUR PRACTICE

We recommend that you use your professional name for your Sole Proprietorship, Professional Corporation (PC), or Professional Limited Liability Company (PLLC). Using your name announces to the public that you are a professional, as opposed to a trade name, such as *We Defend Your Rights.* You can combine your name with the type of law you practice, making it easier for potential clients to find you when using search engines. As an example, my practice name is *Kopf Healthcare Law, LLC.* Including your name increases the likelihood that someone else is not using the practice name you want to use.

Do your due diligence. Thoroughly and deeply investigate, using large search engines, such as Google and your state's database, to confirm the name is not used by someone else in your state, the United States, or internationally. If the name is already in use, it is their property. Established or large law practices will not want you to use their name and may contact you to cease using it. If you use your name only, you can also use a more descriptive trade name. You must also research trade names. You'll want to know names that are allowed (or specifically disallowed) by your state and the rules for registering your name in the state.

To express the essence of your practice, you may add a tag line under your name or trade name on professional letterhead stationery, business cards, and website. For example, my tag line is *Health Law for Health Professionals.* The laws of your state determine the name of your law practice and whether you can have a trade name.

A PC or PLLC may limit your liability.

WHAT FORM WILL YOUR PRACTICE TAKE?

Understanding the advantages and disadvantages of sole proprietorship, PC, or PLLC is essential, and it is discussed below.

SOLE PROPRIETORSHIP

One of your first decisions when forming your solo practice is whether to incorporate. If you are planning to start practicing alone, you can "hang out your shingle" and start work as a Sole Proprietor. A Sole Proprietorship is not a corporate structure.

Advantages

- No fees or legal filing are needed. You are the only owner and often only employee. Many attorneys start out as sole proprietorships and incorporate at a later date.
- You are taxed as self-employed.
- PLLC taxes are often filed with your personal taxes. You do not need separate corporate tax filing and accounting costs.
    - You can obtain an EIN.
    - You can deduct business expenses from your business income, as with the other corporate structures.
- There is no annual meeting or minutes requirement.

Disadvantages

- No protection of your personal assets if sued. You will be personally liable for all debts of the business.
- It may convey to the public a different level of professionalism than a PLLC or PC.
- Tax benefits may be less than a PLLC – seek advice from your accountant.

WHY INCORPORATE?

There are many good reasons to incorporate. The primary reason is the protection of your personal assets and the tax advantages. Just as you have a professional duty to your clients, as a Shareholder or Member of your corporation, you will have a fiduciary duty to your corporation. This duty is the legal obligation to act in the best interests of your company. If your corporation is perfected (more on that later), it can offer the legal protection of your personal assets from lawsuits. These lawsuits do not have to be for malpractice; they could be from an auto accident or divorce, too. If your corporation is not perfected, it may not give you legal protection. The "corporate veil" (see below) can be pierced, and your personal assets may be at risk.

Most states allow attorneys to form a Professional Limited Liability Company (PLLC) or a Professional Corporation (PC). Each state has its own corporate suffix options and statutes. You may be able to choose from a Professional Corporation (PC), Professional Association (PA), Chartered (CHTD) or Limited (LTD). Your state laws, regulations, and tax laws govern professional businesses.

PROFESSIONAL CORPORATION (PC)

Advantages

- The common corporation for a professional is the PC business structure. It has been proven in court for many years to protect your personal assets.
- A corporation is a separate entity from the individual or individuals who are owners or employed by it. It has a separate legal status and rights that an individual or sole proprietor does not have. This is known as the "corporate veil" that separates the corporation from the owner. A corporation can sue someone or another entity, enter into contracts, and incur its own debts and obligations.
- A PC can have a single owner or shareholder, you, and you can be the only employee.

- A PC announces to the public that you are a corporation, not an individual. It is a public perception that an incorporated practice is a more serious professional practice than a non-incorporated practice, even though there are excellent attorneys who are sole proprietors and not incorporated. If there is a lawsuit against you, the corporation can protect you, limit your personal liability and pay damages assessed unless your corporation is not perfected, not in good standing or if gross negligence or intent to commit a crime is found.
- Legal protection of your personal assets is the main reason people become a PC. However, if your corporation is not perfected, is not in good standing and/or does not have the related PC documents and related business accounts (such as the Bylaws, Shareholder Agreement, Employment Contract, business bank account and federal EIN), it will not give you the legal protection you seek. This is also known as "piercing the corporate veil." Therefore, you may want to work with an attorney whose practice includes incorporating clients to make sure your corporation, with the additional documents and steps necessary, is correctly set up under your state laws.
- A PC business structure can protect your personal assets if your corporation is perfected, and you can show that you are conducting a valid business, not just "in name only." "In name only" can occur if you only filed your corporation online or filed Articles of Incorporation only and paid the state fee. It is also known as a sham corporation. Functioning businesses have clients, bank accounts, bookkeeping, tax returns in the corporate name, websites, as well as other evidence of business activities.
- Your state will have well-defined laws about professional corporations, such as formation, permitted corporate activities, corporate

share limitations and closure. You will need to be familiar with these laws.

- A PC can offer you a tax advantage to claim business expenses such as rent or ownership fees, office supplies and equipment, software, technology support, professional liability insurance, license fees and professional membership dues (e.g., TAANA), related to your practice. There are other tax advantages depending upon your personal situation or if you are a C or S corporation. C corporations file taxes separately from their owners, while S corporations can opt to file taxes with their owners' personal tax return. Seek advice from a skilled accountant to decide which is better for you. Generally, the designation of a C or S corporation can be done at a time other than at incorporation.

Disadvantages

- If your corporation is not perfected or incorrectly filed, your personal assets are at risk if you are sued. A lawsuit can occur from multiple sources, such as professional matters, divorce or an auto accident, where the other party thinks you have deep pockets by virtue of being a lawyer.
- Part of corporate perfection involves completing your annual filing and paying your yearly state fees to maintain your corporation's good standing. This allows you to have certain legal and financial benefits. The state fee is usually the same for PCs and PLLCs.
- A PC has separate accounting costs and tax consequences. The amount depends on your tax accountant and state laws.
- You will be required to write and record annual minutes at an annual meeting. It is good business practice to do a yearly overview of actions taken, large purchases, office staff or location changes. These minutes

do not have to be lengthy. PCs often schedule the annual meeting for December 31.

PROFESSIONAL LIMITED LIABILITY COMPANY (PLLC)

Advantages

A PLLC is also a common corporate entity for solo lawyers. Its ability to provide corporate protection has not been tested in court as extensively as the PC.

- A corporation is a separate entity from the individual or individuals who are owners and employed by it. It has a separate legal status and rights that an individual or sole proprietor does not have. This is known as the "corporate veil" that separates the corporation from the owner. A corporation can sue someone or another entity, enter into contracts, and incur its own debts and obligations.
- A PLLC can have one single owner or shareholder, you, who can also be the only employee.
- It announces to the public that you are a type of company, not an individual. It is an indication to the public that you are serious about your work and working as a professional. If there is a lawsuit against you, the corporation can protect you, limit your personal liability, and pay damages unless your corporation is not perfected, is not in good standing or if gross negligence or intent to commit a crime is found.
- Many law practices and firms are PLLCs.
    - A PLLC can also have a single owner or Member with yourself as the only employee.
    - Your state will have well-defined laws about professional limited liability companies (PLLC). These include laws governing formation, permitted corporate activities, share limitations and closure.

   - A PLLC potentially offers the limited liability protection of your personal assets with simpler tax filing than a PC.
   - PLLC taxes are often filed with your personal taxes. You do not need separate corporate tax filing and accounting costs.
   - A PLLC is a separate entity from the individual who is employed by it. It has a separate legal status and rights that an individual or sole proprietor does not have. This is known as the "corporate veil" that separates the corporation from the owner. A PLLC can sue someone or another entity, enter into contracts, and incur its own debts and obligations.
- Legal protection of your personal assets is the main reason people become a PLLC. <u>However,</u> if your PLLC is not in good standing, is not perfected and/or does not have the related documents (such as the Operating Agreement or Employment contract), it will not give you the legal protection you seek. This is known as "piercing the corporate veil." Therefore, you may want to work with an attorney whose practice includes incorporating clients to make sure your corporation, with the additional documents and steps necessary, is set up correctly under your state laws.
- A PLLC business structure can protect your personal assets <u>if</u> your corporation is perfected, and you can show that you are conducting a valid business, not just "in name only." "In name only" can occur if you only filed your corporation online or filed Articles of Incorporation only and paid the state fee. It is also known as a sham corporation. Functioning businesses have clients, bank accounts, bookkeeping, tax returns in the corporate name, websites, as well as other evidence of business activities.
- A PLCC can offer you a tax advantage to claim business expenses, such as rent or ownership fees, office supplies and equipment, software, technology support, professional liability insurance, license fees

and professional membership dues (e.g., TAANA) related to your practice. There are other tax advantages depending upon your personal situation or if your PLLC is designated as a C or S corporation for tax purposes. C corporations file taxes separately from their owners, while S corporations can opt to file taxes with their owners' personal tax return. Seek advice from your accountant on which is better for you. Generally, the designation of a C or S corporation can be done at a time other than at incorporation.

- There is no annual meeting or minutes requirement with PLLC.

Disadvantages

You must complete your annual report and pay your yearly state fees to keep your PLLC in good standing with the state and have legal and financial benefits. The fees for PC or PLLC are usually the same amount.

- PLLCs do not have the same years of court records for personal assets protection as PCs, but still offer limited liability protection for your personal assets if your PLLC is in good standing and perfected. However, if your company is not perfected, it will not give you the legal protection you seek.

PERFECTING YOUR PC OR PLLC

Perfecting your PC or PLLC is a legal term of art that refers to completing the legal and business steps that, if challenged, show your company is a valid business and not a sham. If your business is challenged, one of the first things opposing counsel will check is to see if your business is in good standing with your state, that you have done your annual filing, paid your annual corporate filing fees, and the Articles of Incorporation or Articles of Organization have been accepted and certified. This is public information easily found online. Functioning businesses have Bylaws, Shareholder Agreements or Operating Agreements, Employment

Agreements, business checking accounts, credit cards, offices, websites, business cards, letterhead, and Employer Identification Numbers (EINs) with the IRS. PCs have separate tax filings. Most of this evidence of a functioning business is easily determined. If your corporation is not "perfected," the corporate veil can be pierced, and you can be held personally liable, and your personal assets may be vulnerable. You want to avoid this.

PROFESSIONAL CORPORATION (PC)

- You need to file Professional Articles of Incorporation with your state department that oversees businesses. There is often a separate chapter in the State Statutes for Professional Corporations. It has some different, but essential, terms other than the common Public Corporation/PC. Request a certified copy for your Corporate Book/records.
- You should have corporate shares. Customarily, the shares are given a $1.00/share value to avoid having to hire an appraiser to determine the value of the shares at the time a new owner joins or there is a sale of the PC. Buy-in and buy-out amounts can also be stated in the Shareholder Agreement.
- As the sole owner, you have full control over the PC by holding all the shares. If another owner joins, you can determine at that time what percentage of control you want to give that new owner.
- You can serve as the Resident Agent for your corporation to avoid paying a third-party Resident Agent fee, unless you do not live in the state where your PC is incorporated. The purpose of the Resident Agent of record is to designate someone to send and receive legal documents to if you cannot be found. There are not many situations in which the Resident Agent will need to receive documents for you. However, some attorneys prefer to have a third-party Resident Agent.
- The address of your PC can be your home address. This will be the address of record. You may want to have a different address to receive

mail and clients. With a business address, you can avoid any unexpected visitors to your home. Consider a USPS Post Office Box address or rent a "virtual" office if you do not want or need to rent a brick-and-mortar office at first. A virtual office is a shared space where you pay rent to use their address, receive your mail, meet with clients, use their conference room, and display a sign with your practice name outside their suite.

- Employment Agreement – Even though you are the only employee, you need to have an Employment Agreement that is customary and standard, as you are an employee of your corporation. It is another indication that you have a functioning business. If and when you hire other attorney employees, you can amend the terms at that time if you want to change the terms or benefits that you have as the owner. It is advised that all employees in the same position have the same or a similar contract. The compensation may vary.
- Shareholders' Agreement – This is another customary document for corporations. This is a helpful document for solo lawyers as it describes the owner's benefits, share value, ownership percentages, restrictions, termination terms, and retirement provisions. If, and when, you add another owner to your corporation, you can amend the terms prior to the offer if you prefer the new owner to have different terms. All shareholders should have the same Agreement. Certain benefits and terms can vary, especially for you as the founding owner.
- Corporate Book with Stock Certificate and Seal – You need to have this official corporate book or digital version with the corporate seal and stock certificates from a legal supply company (e.g., Blumberg Excelsior, Inc. at www.bloomberg.com). The Corporate Book will hold the original certified and sealed Articles of Incorporation, other filings, EIN document, your employment agreement, shareholder agreement, corporate minutes, stock certificates, and stock register.

- Once the state confirms your incorporation, you should draft your first organizational meeting minutes.
- You have a year from the incorporation confirmation to complete all the documents.

PROFESSIONAL LIMITED LIABILITY COMPANY (PLLC)

You must file Professional Articles of Organization with your state department that oversees businesses. Request a certified copy for your Corporate Book.

- You can have company shares. Customarily, the shares are given a $1.00/share value to avoid having to hire an appraiser to determine the value of the shares at the time a new Member joins the PLLC, or when it is sold. Buy-in and buy-out amounts can be stated in the Operating Agreement.
- As the sole Member/owner, you have complete control over the PLLC by holding all the shares. If another owner joins, you can determine at that time what percentage of control you want to give that new owner.
- You can become the Resident Agent for your corporation to avoid paying a third-party Resident Agent fee, unless you do not live in the state where your PLLC is incorporated. The purpose of the Resident Agent of record is to have someone designated to send and receive legal documents if you cannot be found. There are not many situations in which the Resident Agent will need to receive documents for you. However, some attorneys prefer to have a third-party Resident Agent.
    - The address of your PC can be your home address. It will be the address of record. You may want to have a different address to receive mail and clients. With a business address, you can avoid any unexpected visitors to your home. Consider a USPS Post Office Box address or rent a "virtual" office if you do not want or need to

rent a brick-and-mortar office at first. A virtual office is a shared space where you pay rent to use their address, receive your mail, meet clients, use their conference room, and display a sign with your practice name outside their suite.

- The Operating Agreement is another customary document for corporations. This is a helpful document for the solo lawyer, as it is in this document that you state your owner's benefits, value of the shares, ownership percentages, restrictions, termination terms, and retirement. If and when you add another Member to your corporation, you can amend the terms at that time before the offer if you prefer the new Member not to have the same terms as you. All shareholders should have the same Agreement. Specific benefits and terms can vary, especially for you as the founding owner.
- Even though you are the only employee, you need to have an Employment Agreement that is customary and standard, as you are an employee of your corporation. It is another indication that you have a functioning business. If and when you hire other attorney employees, you can amend the terms at that time if you want to change the terms or benefits that you have as the owner. It is advised that all employees in the same position have the same or a similar contract. The compensation may vary.
- You need to have an official Corporate Book with Stock Certificate and Seal (or digital version with the corporate seal and stock certificates). Obtain this from a legal supply company (e.g., Blumberg Excelsior, Inc. at www.bloomberg.com). The Corporate Book will hold the original certified and sealed Articles of Incorporation, other filings, EIN document, your employment agreement, your Operating Agreement, stock certificates and stock register. You have one year to complete all the documents.

FILE FOR A FEDERAL EMPLOYER IDENTIFICATION NUMBER (EIN) WITH THE IRS

This is a federal tax identification number for your practice. It is easy to apply online at www.IRS.gov. It is preferable to have an EIN for your taxes, and if your clients or other requesting parties ask for it for their taxes, a 1099 or a W-9. A PC requires an EIN to file for its taxes, but a PLLC does not require an EIN for its tax filing. You can use your Social Security number to create a PLLC. However, we recommend that you get an EIN for the PLLC so you do not have to give out your Social Security number to your clients or other requesting parties. It is also more professional. There are a few exceptions when you need to have an EIN with a PLLC. Otherwise, you can use your Social Security number if you do not get an EIN.

OTHER FILINGS

- Your trade name is important. First, check if your state allows attorneys to practice under a trade name. Then, do a deep search to see if your proposed trade name is available and there is not a similar name that could be considered substantially the same. Register the trade name with your state. See state laws regarding this matter.
- Register with the state if you are "Doing Business As" (DBA) a name other than your corporate or company name.

CONSULTATION WITH AN ACCOUNTANT

A skilled tax accountant can be an invaluable addition to your corporation. Tax accountants assist with:

- Tax implications and determination of the type of corporation (C or S), individual, or joint tax filing.
- Accounting costs for PC, PLLC, or Sole Proprietorship tax filings.
- Estimated yearly accounting expenses and taxes.

ADDITIONAL IMPORTANT ACTIONS TO DO WHEN SETTING UP A SOLO LAW PRACTICE

- Open a bank account(s) in the practice's name. Consider a checking account for operational expenses, a Client Trust fund or Interest on Lawyers Trust Accounts (IOLTA), a savings account, or a money market. To avoid unintentional and costly oversights, refer to your state's laws for rules about banking requirements.
- Deposit a substantial amount of funds as your start-up capital in your new solo practice bank account. Start-up capital is designed to separate start-up expenses from your personal expenses. Start-up expenses may include legal fees, insurance, marketing (hard copy and digital), filing fees, computer, laptop, smart phone and service, computer cameras, lighting, and background considerations (e.g., for virtual meeting programs such as Zoom and Microsoft Teams), internet service and routers, multifunction machine, office phone services and printer equipment, programs, practice management software, consultants, and office supplies.
- Establish a solo practice phone number. This may be a landline or cell phone. Obtain phone-related services such as transcribed voice mail to email or text, forwarding of calls to other numbers and devices, an off-site or virtual phone receptionist, and the ability to call from your cell phone, showing the caller as your practice caller identification (CID) number instead of your personal cell phone number.
- Register a domain name for your practice website.
- Work with a developer on this website.
- Check with an attorney with experience with professional websites to confirm that your site complies with your state and federal laws governing attorney websites.
- Purchase professional liability insurance, cyber security insurance, and umbrella insurance. Consider part-time insurance that may be

available when you start up if you are not working more than 20 hours a week. Ask your colleagues and state Bar Associations for recommendations.

- Find office space. Initially, consider subleasing space with other attorneys who can give you legal and moral support. Your local Bar Association often advertises these opportunities. Other options are virtual practice (no brick-and-mortar office) and executive suite offices. Many attorneys have moved to a home office and practice online. There are pros and cons to this situation that vary with your living space options, your client obligations, the type of law you practice, and interactions with those living with you, including canine or feline household pets.
- Keep a record of all expenses related to setting up your practice.
- Review your state guidelines and professional code of conduct for attorneys in private practice.
- Consider practice management software that includes integration of posting client information to all programs including payments, contacts list, time entries, billing, client funds, payments, produces the bill, emails bills, general ledger of all income and costs for end of year tax filing (examples are Software Technology, LLC (STI), integrated or individual programs such as Practice Manager, Tabs and General Ledger, Amicus Attorney, PCLaw, CLIO, Abacus Law, and Time Matters). Consult your colleagues and the Bar Association for recommendations. An electronic practice management system fully allows you, the solo lawyer, to do it all yourself and perhaps avoid hiring a secretary, billing company, or other services.
- Obtain or develop practice document templates for your engagement letter (with fees, retainers or advance payments and office policies), and Attorney HIPAA Business Associate Agreement (needed if you hold medical information or personal health information (PHI)).

- Establish support relationships with Information Technology (IT) and cybersecurity companies. These are essential to getting you back up and working when your computer and other electronic devices malfunction, have glitches, or lose data. It is impractical to work in our legal system without dependable support for electronic devices, computers/laptops, internet service, smartphones, electronic notifications, email, and calendar.
- Obtain business plan agreements for your internet, computer, and phone services. You will get better service than a residential plan when there is a problem, and those companies usually offer helpful business services, such as visual voicemail to your smartphone and other digital support services, to make your life as a solo much easier. Look into the largest companies in your area that provide the most reliable, fast internet, repair services, and business-friendly support services.
- Establish a merchant services account for credit card payments with your bank or LawPay. It is essential today to have this for clients' payments. You must do an annual Payment Card Data Security (PCI) compliance report. Beware of security issues related to credit cards. Do not enter credit card information for your clients or retain their card numbers in your files because of the increased liability.
- Identify an attorney who will cover for you if you are not available due to a medical emergency or if there are times you just cannot work or answer client calls or emails. The TAANA network is a good place to start!

If your law practice does not include corporate law pertaining to incorporation and setting up a practice, we recommend you work with an attorney who is very familiar with these matters to ensure you get started in the right direction and that your corporation will be "perfected." Avoid online "corporations in a box" offers, as they often do not comply with your state incorporation laws and professional rules.

You will decide the scope, depth, and goal of your solo practice and form your business the way you envision your practice. As your practice grows, you can increase, decrease or expand services. Consult experienced solo attorneys and accountants. Join your Bar Association and other legal associations, such as the Solo Practice Sections of TAANA.

Remember. You are in control.

CHAPTER 2

Opening a Law Office

Randi Kopf, RN, MS, JD

DISCLOSURE

THE AUTHOR HAS NO FINANCIAL INTERESTS OR RELATIONSHIPS WITH ANY OF THE PRODUCTS OR PROGRAMS SUGGESTED IN THIS CHAPTER, NOR DO THEY ENDORSE THEM.

DISCLAIMER

WHILE THIS CHAPTER GUIDEBOOK OFFERS GUIDANCE ON SOLO PRACTICE, IT SHOULD NOT BE CONSTRUED AS LEGAL ADVICE.

TO BEGIN: HOW DO YOU FORESEE YOUR LEGAL PRACTICE?

What type of law do you want to practice? Litigation, administrative, contractual, transactional, governmental, general practice, a specific area of law you like?

- How do you want to practice law? The joy of private practice is that you can do it your way.
- Think about your lifestyle, your financial assets and needs, and the realistic time available between home, family, and work.
- Workdays and times. 9:00 am–5:00 pm? 11:00 am–7:00 pm? What about working nights, on weekends, holidays, or while on vacation?
- Will you work full-time or part-time?
- What should your workspace look like? Is it your own office, a shared suite, alone or with limited staff support, a home office with remote access, or another configuration that will best support your needs?
- Will your practice be paperless, all electronic, or would you prefer paper files too?

- What are your overall financial goals? Include start-up capital and ongoing overhead expenses in your plan. What do you want or need to earn?
- Will you practice solo with or without any assistants or other legal associates (attorneys or paralegals), or solo but within a larger law office with other unaffiliated attorneys?
- Who and where are your target clients?
- Estimate what it will cost you to open your "doors." Be precise and as inclusive as you can imagine.
- Realistically determine what you can afford, how much money you will need, and whether you need a loan.

GETTING INTO THE DETAILS

Your Law Office

- Office location: should your office be near your target clients and/or your home?
- Transportation to the office. How will clients get to your office? How will you get to the office?
    - Disability access
    - Parking ease (for you and clients)
- Will you buy or rent private office or suite space, share space in another law practice, use executive office space, rent a separate brick-and-mortar office, have a fully virtual law practice (check your state laws), or work at home with remote access?
    - Remember to ask yourself what you realistically can afford. Where will you obtain start-up money?

CONSIDER ALL OFFICE EXPENSES (FIXED AND VARIABLE)

- Professional liability insurance (legal and nursing)
- Rent

- Utilities
- Security monitoring
- Cybersecurity insurance
- Legal research program fees (in-person or virtual services such as LexisNexis, Fast Case, Westlaw, Bloomberg Law)
- Technology & Cybersecurity support costs can be your most considerable ongoing cost as these services are essential to keep you in practice and online, monitor security concerns, virus and malware alerts, fix glitches and malfunctioning programs, and restore computer crashes.
- Bar membership
- Licenses (legal and nursing)
- CLE
- Parking
- Housekeeping
- If you want to (or need to) have a home office, include the above costs plus
- Costs related to a home office, such as percentage utilities, rent/mortgage
    - Phone, internet, cable, and cell access
    - Printing, scanning, fax
    - Remote access to office computer
    - Consult your tax accountant regarding any tax benefits or liabilities

SERVICES

Internet, Wi-Fi

- Phones
- Mobile phone
- Fax
- Answering service
- Visual (transcribed) voice mail

- USPS mailing programs, Fed Ex and/or UPS account and "you print" mailing labels
- Technology support
- Security for office space (locked doors and or file cabinets) security alarm system

SUPPLIES & EQUIPMENT

- Furniture and fireproof safe/filing cabinets
- Hardware
- Computers
    - Desktop, monitors, laptop or tablet (when away from your workspace)
    - Scanner
    - Fax
    - Printer (black and white laser or color) and/or multifunction machine (copier, fax, also backup printer and scanner)
    - Wi-Fi routers and extenders, private server
    - Shredder
    - Computer camera, lighting, and background
    - Digital storage devices, thumb drives, external hard drives, CDs
    - USB port extender
    - APC (American Power Conversion) battery backup
    - Surge protectors
- Telephone Services
- Smartphones
    - Voice Over Internet Protocol (VOIP) phone service with unlimited calling
    - Hands-free telephone system with message options
    - Conference calling
    - Remote access

    - Receptionist on phone system
    - Forwarding of calls
    - Ability to call from your cell phone with your office phone Caller ID
    - Wireless headsets and other available devices
- Office Supplies (even paperless offices use some paper products)
- Letterhead
    - Legal pads
    - Tabs
    - Sticky notes
    - Pens
    - Highlighters
    - Stapler
    - "File Copy" and "Private and Confidential" stampers
    - Exhibit tabs
    - Red ropes, file folders and labels
    - Practice mailing labels
    - Envelopes
    - Paper and binder clips
    - Business cards

COMPUTERS AND ELECTRONICS

- Technical advisors and IT support services, web designer, web host, cyber security support team
- Programs
- Most current Apple or Mac programs (at this writing, MS Office 365, and Pages, Numbers, and Keynote for Mac),
    - Law practice management programs that include time management, client files, email storage, calendar, document management. Examples are DocuSign, eSign or other electronic signature

service, office productivity and billing software, and their support services, such as Software Technology, LLC (STI) integrated or individual programs (Practice Manager, Tabs, General Ledger), Amicus Attorney, PC Law, CLIO, Abacus Law, Time Matters

- Client portal and encrypted email services
- Legal research tools such as Lexis Nexis, Westlaw, Bloomberg Law, Fast Case
- Web hosting company,
- Adobe Acrobat to convert PDF documents
- Litera – document compare program
- Zoom, Citrix, or other visual conference program,
- Merchant services at banks are safest at this time. VENMO or ZELLE are not advised for business use, as they have had fraud and privacy issues
- Credit card payment system, such as LawPay, Tabs3Pay – integrated into your practice management programs
- Cloud storage and off-site backup, such as Carbonite or MS360 – HIPAA compliant or to protect attorney-client privileged information
- Secure remote access to your business computers (Go To My PC or LogMeIn)
- Antivirus, malware, and spam protection, digital protection, hacking monitoring service, breach and attack alerts (Webroot, Sentinel One, MS Security)
- Security program and monitoring for all devices used for work
- Domain name, website, business email addresses

- Social media presence, updating, monitoring, and reports
- Artificial Intelligence (AI) systems are rapidly developing to build entirely new smart applications.

FINANCES

- Startup capital to pay for corporate filings and expenses to be deposited into your new business bank account
  - Startup capital to pay for corporate filings and expenses to be deposited into your new business bank account
  - Income (payments to yourself)
  - Monthly expenses (estimate rent, phones, internet, utilities, insurances, and other monthly costs)
- Cash flow. Consider additional income streams at the start, for example, contract work, presentations to target client organizations, teaching, writing, part-time positions, court-appointed panels such as guardianship, mediation, pro bono, criminal defense, and referrals from colleagues or client target entities you may have advised or performed pro bono work
- Pro Bono to generate future income and name recognition
  - Bar Associations
  - Client organizations
  - Community Service
  - Lectures
  - Webinars
  - Write articles/posts (for example, "Ask the Lawyer" columns)
  - Attending conferences
  - Savings, money market, and retirement accounts (speak with your accountant or financial advisor about a SEP or IRA (also ROTH IRA), and other financial vehicles).

CONFIDENTIALITY AND SECURITY

Electronic Security Plan actions for all media data, computer, all electronic equipment, phones, and files

- Locked doors and file cabinets
- Offsite, continuous, and monitored by a security firm (Sensei), cloud-based, secure computer system backup in case of disaster
  - Carbonite or MS360 (is also HIPAA compliant)
  - Additional HIPAA and HIPAA Security Rules requirements if you hold PHI
    - Work with your IT support people to develop electronic security and privacy protections for your computer data, Wi-Fi, software, and documents, control access to computers, antivirus, malware, and take steps to safeguard sensitive information to protect attorney-client privilege and avoid inadvertent disclosures
    - American Power Conversion (APC) battery backup units for the protection of your computer, phone systems, electronic equipment, and all office machine equipment.
- Substantial surge protectors for all electronics

THIRD-PARTY CONTRACTORS

You may want to add these services depending upon your need:

- Business lawyer
- Accountant
- Insurance broker
  - Professional liability
  - Umbrella overhead for office
  - To cover computer and office equipment hard and software
- Cyber security insurance
- IT Support
  - Cybersecurity support
  - Support or legal staff – in person or virtual
  - Internet, WiFi, and phone service (cell and landline) providers
  - Web designer and hosting services

- Social media support
- Printing company
- Office supplies vendor accounts (Staples, Amazon, Costco)
- Offsite support staff
- Legal research service
- Payment or billing services
- Offsite back up service

BEFORE YOUR FIRST CLIENT

- Consider how you will establish in-person and virtual client relationships
- Determine the legal services you will offer
- Decide your fee structures
- Create a client intake form
- Draft your Engagement letter
- Review your state statutes for legal practice
- Be aware of your state's professional code

BE ADVISED

It is imperative in law practice to protect your client's information and client confidentiality. Keep current with scams that could invade your systems and lock you out, breach attorney-client privilege from hacking, and inappropriate disclosure. Unintentional electronic communications via email or text can be a serious professional violation. Emails and texts are not confidential. Be aware that some smartphone communications, data, and internet services are easily intercepted or compromised. Take all steps available to you that are advised by the Bar Associations, Professional Associations, and case law to protect your client's information. There have been cases of lawyers being sued by clients whose confidential information was stolen, resulting in bad outcomes, client lawsuits, business or employment-related negotiations, divorce-related matters, or other material client matters. Plan, act, and document your cybersecurity efforts.

CHAPTER 3

Marketing

Randi Kopf, RN, MS, JD

DISCLOSURE

THE AUTHOR HAS NO FINANCIAL INTERESTS OR RELATIONSHIPS WITH ANY OF THE PRODUCTS OR PROGRAMS SUGGESTED IN THIS CHAPTER, NOR DO THEY ENDORSE THEM.

DISCLAIMER

WHILE THIS CHAPTER GUIDEBOOK OFFERS GUIDANCE ON SOLO PRACTICE, IT SHOULD NOT BE CONSTRUED AS LEGAL ADVICE.

This chapter covers marketing basics when setting up your solo law practice. The goal of marketing is to give potential clients an impression of your experience and success.

Once you have determined your target marketing audience, consider tailoring these marketing action items to your budget and your practice timeline.

STATE, FEDERAL AND PROFESSIONAL ETHICS RULES

Caveat #1! Lawyer websites are governed by state and federal law, published professional codes, rules, ethics opinions, and guidelines. Before you get too far into your marketing plan, website, and social media development, check your state laws and professional codes or opinions that govern and regulate lawyers' advertising, websites, and social media presence. There are a few jurisdictions that do not want your website to advertise to their citizens; there may be disclaimers to be added, and advertising rules to be followed. For example, the State of Maryland requires a copy of your advertisement or marketing materials, including your website, to be kept for at least three years, with records of when and where it was made available. Many states require an easy-to-read advertising statement for the public: "This website is intended as an attorney advertisement." There have been successful lawsuits against attorney websites for multiple violations, such as using the website for unlawful or unprofessional purposes, making false and misleading statements (e.g., "You will be happy with my results"), listing educational or certificate credentials you have not earned, and not complying with State or Federal law.

- Caveat #2! Although at the writing of this chapter in 2025, AI (Artificial Intelligence) is emerging as a valuable tool for writing and decision making, it does not yet have experience with what is appropriate for attorney marketing that complies with customary and standard professional standards. Currently, it can "hallucinate" or falsely create legal citations or references. Because current iterations of AI want to provide you with an answer, it can make up or create false information. AI will "learn" to provide unlimited writing options. However, be very careful how you utilize this exciting software, especially when using it to create marketing materials, a resume, or email text. Until the process is refined, use AI as a creative consultant, not as the final word.

WHAT IS INCLUDED IN ATTORNEY PRACTICE MARKETING?

- Your email signature, font, award badges, and association logos
- Your digital and physical business card
- Letterhead, return envelope address, and paper used for hard copies
- Your website, social media presence, postings
- Your practice logo
- Your trade name and or tag line

- Website advertisements, such as TAANA's lawyer referral page
- Presenting lectures, seminars, and webinars
- Writing and posting articles about your law specialty
- In-person and virtual networking
- Attending Bar meetings, social events, and conferences
- Attending target client conferences, such as purchasing a vendor table
- Sponsoring an event
- Selective online or newsletter advertising

LETTERHEADS, ENVELOPES, AND BUSINESS CARDS

Letterheads, envelopes and business cards are part of your professional image. You can design them on your computer and print them on your printer if needed. However, professionally printed letterheads and envelopes can save more time than your lost income creating them and presenting a more professional image. Consider the font, paper color, embossed print, and paper weight of your professional stationery and card stock for your business cards. It all says something about you. For example, most law firms use black ink, white paper, strong fonts like Times Roman, and heavyweight paper (over 20 lbs.) As a solo, consider using a unique, but easily readable colored ink on ivory paper. Using a strong but different font will stand out. You can add award badges and logos to your sites and signatures. This change can send subtle or powerful messages that you are an individual and as effective as a larger firm. Think outside the traditional box.

- Business cards are still used, especially in a conference setting, social gathering, or when you meet someone unexpectedly, such as on vacation or at a neighborhood store. Always have some business cards stashed somewhere on your person. Keep one or two in your wallet or pocket. Carry your cards even on vacation or when doing errands. You never know when you might need it. Business cards travel easily from person to person. You can hire a designer for your cards or do it yourself. Again, compare the business cards that you have seen or received. What is it about the ones you like that makes you feel good about the attorney? Notice why this feature stands out to you.

- Consider adding a tag line under your name on your website, social media, business card, and professional letterhead, such as "Nurse Attorney – Protecting Healthcare Professionals," or designing a practice logo as part of your professional image. Collaborate with an experienced designer to ensure the logo loads smoothly on mobile devices. Remember to conduct a trademark search of the potential tagline or logo you want to use and make sure it is not already in use. You do not want legal action against you when your practice becomes successful enough to pay damages to someone or a corporation that had the logo or tag line before you. An Intellectual Property attorney can help you with trademark questions.
- Although many smartphones can transfer or send business card information immediately, there can be confidentiality issues with phone-to-phone transfers, especially when tapping another phone to transfer information. You can also transfer private information or introduce malware to your phone.

OTHER MARKETING OPTIONS

- Successful marketing options include offering organizations or businesses with potential clients free or minimal payment virtual or in-person webinars and presentations on topics that will attract potential clients' interest. This is an excellent way to get name recognition and an opportunity to show your expertise. You can create your own webinars for marketing use.

- Write, or offer to write, a brief article for newspapers, online newsletters, professional journals, and newsletters. Offer to write professional and specialty resources on a current topic in your area of law. These kinds of publications could bring you potential clients and get you noticed by other referral attorneys. Examples are "Managing Bankruptcy During a National Crisis" or "How to Protect Your Personal Information in Your Online Medical Records." Post these articles on your website and social media.
- At the beginning of your solo practice, you will find that free or pro bono work will introduce the community to you and your area of law for referrals and to new clients. This pro bono period does not have to last years, but it will pay off. Even the most successful established lawyers continue to do some. It is part of the capital investment in your practice and needs to be ongoing. These expenses may be a tax deduction, so consult your tax preparer or accountant.
- Networking is an effective marketing strategy, both in person and online, for enhancing name recognition, generating referrals, fostering collaborations, securing new employment opportunities, and expanding professional contacts. Attend Bar Association meetings, events, social events, and celebrations, and give out those business cards. Target professional organizations, such as TAANA, American Health Law Association (AHLA), and American Association for Justice (formerly Association of Trial Attorneys or ATLA), to attend meetings and virtual meeting calls. Subscribe to or join pertinent listservs and contribute when you can to show your subject expertise.
- If there is an in-person or online conference by an organization that serves your target client base or is especially related to your area of practice, consider sponsoring an event, purchasing program advertising, or leasing a vendor table. Be prepared to give your quick description of who you are, what you can do for them, and why they should

work with you. Consider imprinting your name on de minimis gifts such as pens, laptop camera lens covers, or flash drives. Offer something that everyone can use, requiring little financial outlay for you.

- Remember to be the professional your prospective clients want to see. Your clothing, attitude, and demeanor all affect the impression you make.

WEBSITE

- Your professional website is your primary source of advertising and marketing today. In many ways, websites have replaced the resume or CV. When potential clients are looking for a particular lawyer, they often turn to a large search engine, such as Google, before asking their friends and colleagues.
- Most attorneys work with a web designer to develop their website. We advise you to work with a web developer who has worked with attorneys and is familiar with the governing professional rules and regulations. Be sure to explain to your developer the impression you want the site to give, the essence of your practice, and the clients you seek to attract. We do not recommend using an inexpensive "do-it-yourself" online website development company. These companies put you at high risk for attorney-client privacy issues since they usually cannot offer professional elements such as site (SSL) locking to secure communication between your browser and the website's server, or registering and protecting your domain name from theft. However, the cost of this service is not an indicator of a more successful site or a better product outcome.
- Ask colleagues, friends, and family about their experiences with websites. If you like a particular site, you can usually find the developer's name at the bottom of the home page, labeled "this site was developed by ____." Web developers possess programming skills that

can enhance the polish of your information's the distribution and optimization, ultimately improving the effectiveness of your website. They can suggest pertinent keywords to use to optimize search results. They will know how to secure your site and social media accounts and posts, add interactive functions, keep your site and social media looking fresh and current, and make your site viewable on all devices and computer systems. A skilled web designer can keep your site current by posting photos, award badges, your YouTube videos, and webinars you've given, posting new content, and suggesting other aspects of the site that will make your website attractive, functional, and meaningful for potential clients to want to visit and engage you as their lawyer.

- Be aware that your email and client contacts on your mobile devices or computers can be hacked and stolen. You are required to take "reasonable" actions to protect client information. Be thoughtful about which apps or websites you give access to this confidential information, such as Zoom, FaceTime, and Google Photos. Your attorney-client privilege extends to your mobile devices and electronic programs you may sign up with and give access to your contacts list and email. Be sure to limit access to this data.
- Generally, visitors prefer to be able to scan your home page or landing page and gather key information about why they should hire you in a few seconds. Consider your tendency when "googling" for information about a physician, plumber, or other service. What causes you to either quickly look at the website and move on or capture your attention to read on? What catches your attention? Use your own experience when developing your own site. If you can capture the potential client's attention, they might click on a link or move to another, more detailed page. Visiting many solo lawyers' websites is a good starting point to get an idea of what you like and dislike. Do not forget colors; the background color of a site sets the stage for

your potential client to feel you are the professional for them. Here is a useful tip: When your site is finished, but before you "go live," send links to several non-legal family and friends and ask them what they think of it. An outside opinion can reveal things you did not intend or which are interpreted very differently from your perspective. For example, a plastic surgeon's website had full-length photographs of naked women patients. When the doctor was asked why they thought it was appropriate, as patients' faces were seen, the physician responded that it was customary for this specialty practice to use these types of photographs. A firm explanation of HIPAA, professional ethics, and potential legal liabilities followed, and the website was improved.

DOMAIN NAME

- Consider a domain name that is your name and/or reflects your legal practice. They are the first words that can catch a potential client's eye when searching for a lawyer. Many lawyers use their name in the domain name plus "law" or a keyword of their practice, such as "health" or "malpractice." It is easier for a potential client to find you if a key descriptive word and your name are in your domain name. Google also uses those words to "find" you for their results list when responding to a person's search.
- You must ensure your selected domain name is not already in use. Remember, www means the World Wide Web, so check beyond your state and even your country. Also consider the "essentially the same" rule (your domain name is so close to another's name that it is "essentially the same" to the public) or if you are misleading the public by its name, such as "USA Law" when you do not practice in every/most states.

DOMAIN NAME REGISTRATION

Once you determine that you can use your domain name, you need to register it with a reliable and reputable company, such as Network Solutions, not a company that offers domain name registration for $10.00 or other very low prices. Do your due diligence and research the company to see if they have privacy complaints or other complaints filed that could be potential liability for you and your professional website. There are multiple domain suffixes available, such as .net or .biz, which can be confusing or misdirect a visitor to a site similar to your name but has nothing to do with you. Be aware of the domain suffix you are purchasing.

SOCIAL MEDIA

Postings on social media accounts are considered advertising by many jurisdictions. Professional grievances have been filed against an attorney's social media postings, blogs, and inappropriate client interactions on these sites. Social media is frequently and successfully used. Be mindful of unintentionally giving legal advice, which is very easy to do. Follow published attorney use guidelines and avoid inappropriate attorney-client conduct. Successful professional grievances have stemmed from social media posts involving pornography, asking clients for social dates in the posting, and other professionally inappropriate content. You need to monitor and control your social media presence. It represents the professional you. All social media that you use needs your close attention, and you should regularly monitor it —your professional reputation is on the line.

WEBSITE HOSTING AND SOCIAL MEDIA MANAGEMENT TEAM

Your hosting and web/social media management team company is separate from the developer and company that you register your domain name with. A reliable, professional, and helpful company is very important. Ask colleagues about their work and also engage with vendors at Bar meetings. Your web host is the one who keeps you online. Your web host protects your website and social media from hackers, attackers, spam, and thieves. Your web host controls your professional email address, your email traffic, and the storage of your email. You need a web host who will be there when you need them. Web hosting can be expensive, but considering what it does for your practice and your sanity, it is worth the investment.

- Your web host and social media management team help you "get the word out" through their programming and content. They will advise you about other successful legal sites and social media they have developed and what made them successful, post new social media content, and suggest other aspects of the site and social media that will make your website and social media attractive and meaningful so that potential clients want to visit and engage you as their lawyer.

YOUR IT SUPPORT COMPANY

Your web hosting company may be part of a larger IT support company that provides multiple services related to your computer services, programs, email, internet, Zoom, and generally everything you need to practice as an attorney today. Select this company with care. They are your life support. For example, after a routine Microsoft program update, my entire system vanished. I had a black screen, no programs, no email, no C drive, and nothing. My website and email (my professional lifelines) were down. I received no email, nor could I email. My IT support people redirected my email until it was working, recovered my "lost" emails, switched my site to a new server, recovered most of my missing emails, reinstalled my programs, and got everything up and running. I had an off-site backup that helped, but that was only half of the problem. If your system lacks the necessary framework to download backed-up files and data, it cannot restore the computer. My IT support team, whom I have worked with for over 20 years, eventually got everything back and held my hand during this very stressful time until all was back up and running. Thank you, ByteRightSupport.com. Select a team that can rescue your computer and your practice in a digital crisis.

ANNOUNCEMENTS

It is still worthwhile to make an announcement, digital and paper, in your local Bar journals, newsletters, law school alumni news, send paper and email announcements to lawyers, businesses, and firms you know or think would have clients to refer to you and post announcements via your blog and/or your social accounts.

CLIENT OUTREACH/DEVELOPMENT

Another aspect of marketing your practice is doing client outreach/ client development. There are several ways to do this.

Calling clients to say hello or congratulate them on a personal event, such as a marriage or a new business opening. You can also do this type of contact by email. Sometimes, a phone call has more impact; it is more effective for a client to hear interest in your voice than simply viewing an electronic message. Send flowers for an office opening or other celebration. Take them out to lunch and avoid discussing business.

- Add a personal note to your billing statement, handwritten, when possible, to show you value that particular client and their challenges, mention progress made on the matter, or their personal celebrations.
- Sending a client survey once a client matter has been closed is another method to improve your practice. You can receive specific

feedback and send the client a message that you care about their opinion of your work. Hopefully, they will refer new clients to you.

- Send holiday and event cards or emails. Most people like to be remembered on New Year's or Thanksgiving. When sending a card, whether electronic or otherwise, include something personal to show you took the time to send it, and it was not just a mass mailing.
- Invite clients to a conference or webinar you are giving.
- Let clients know when you've been published, or mentioned in a newspaper or online journal or send a copy or link to the article or book, or when you made a significant legal achievement that is now public, such as contributing to newly revised law, were recognized as a Super Lawyer or America's Most Honored Professional, won a case that will be of interest to them or will potentially impact future matters for your clients.

PROTECT YOUR INTELLECTUAL PROPERTY (IP)

It is very important that you protect your hard work and investment into your new practice by copyrighting and/or trademarking your logo and other proprietary work product, articles or images you post on your website or social media or included in your mailings (hard copy or electronic) or de minimis items given out. We recommend giving notice of ownership by using your "common law" copyright. You can easily do this by adding to the bottom of a written page, website, or webinar page, the recognized copyright symbol ©, your name or practice name, and the year the material was first published. For example, my common law copyright is © *Copyright Kopf HealthLaw, LLC 2025.* This form of copyright acts to claim ownership of the text and images by your corporation or you. Hopefully, it will be a deterrent to visitors stealing and plagiarizing your work product. It is worthwhile to have minimal protection of your intellectual property.

- Common law copyright is not the formal copyright filed with the US Copyright Office or a trademark with the United States Patent and Trademark Office. If you want full legal protection of your intellectual property filed with the US government offices and to avoid an infringement action against you for unauthorized use of copyrighted material or trademarks, it is best to seek counsel from an experienced intellectual property lawyer or copyright and trademark attorney. We do not recommend that you file a copyright or trademark yourself. It can be complicated and carries potentially heavy legal ramifications and or financial damages.

BEFORE YOU MOVE ON ...

Draft a plan for your new practice, including all the factors described in Chapters 1–3.

CHAPTER 4

Scope of Practice

Teressa Sanzio, RN, MPA, JD

DISCLOSURE

THE AUTHOR HAS NO FINANCIAL INTERESTS OR RELATIONSHIPS WITH ANY OF THE PRODUCTS OR PROGRAMS SUGGESTED IN THIS CHAPTER, NOR DO THEY ENDORSE THEM.

DISCLAIMER

WHILE THIS CHAPTER GUIDEBOOK OFFERS GUIDANCE ON SOLO PRACTICE, IT SHOULD NOT BE CONSTRUED AS LEGAL ADVICE.

CLIENT SELECTION

Selecting clients is just as crucial for the attorney as it is for clients selecting an attorney. There should be a good professional fit. For more details about the client selection criteria, please refer to Chapter 7.

This chapter will discuss the logistics of client selection before starting representation.

PERFORMING A CONFLICT CHECK

Having a system in place to check for conflicts is typically mandated by most professional insurance liability carriers and policies. As an attorney, and consistent with the professional code of conduct, your loyalty and fiduciary duty are to your existing clients. In anticipation of representing a new client, it is necessary to determine if a conflict exists with your current clients before initiating representation. If a conflict exists, whether potential or perceived, you have to obtain informed written consent from both the current client and the potential new client before commencing representation of the new client. Each practitioner should verify with the Rules of Professional Responsibility in their respective states.

INITIAL CONSULTATIONS

- The initial interview with a potential new client is critical.
- First, determine if a client is already represented. There are occasions when potential clients are not satisfied with their current attorneys and contact you to inquire about how you would handle their case differently. This may appear to be a "curb-side" second opinion; however, you cannot provide legal advice to anyone that you do not represent. If the potential new client is currently represented, do not engage in further dialogue with that person until the issues with the current attorney are resolved, or the current attorney and potential client's relationship is terminated.
- Use the initial consultation to discuss general process questions only, and it should not involve rendering legal advice. During this consultation, the client should be able to discern the attorney's knowledge of the issues presented and experience in working in that area of law. During the initial consultation, the attorney should discuss fees and discern the client's ability to pay for legal services.
- Attorneys can offer a free initial consultation or charge for it. You can conduct consultations in person or by telephone. The attorney and the potential client can then determine whether to proceed with the attorney-client relationship.
- During this interview, first assess the client's ability to comprehend the legal process and the need to manage their expectations. Perhaps the client's expectations are unrealistic, and no matter what assistance is provided, the result they "expect" will not likely happen. If you do not address this issue at the outset, and the client does not receive the

expected results, future potential problems may arise, such as a bar complaint or a lawsuit.

- Second, the potential new client must understand their obligation to be truthful throughout litigation. Once the client understands the concept of attorney-client privilege, being completely forthcoming is less of a challenge. Further, the attorney-client relationship will have a solid foundation. Should the attorney-client relationship deteriorate during the pending litigation, and should the client lose trust in the attorney's capabilities or the attorney's advocacy for the client, the attorney should consider withdrawing from further representation.

SCOPE OF REPRESENTATION

The professional rules of conduct require attorneys to be competent to practice in a specific area of law. Handling a legal matter for a potential client that is outside one's area of expertise or experience can be problematic. If, however, you decide to assist the client, you must disclose to the client that you have limited or no experience in the area of law. This may not matter to the client, but the disclosure, nonetheless, is critical. For example, a potential client asks for assistance with a divorce, but you are not familiar with this area of law. You should disclose that you are certainly not opposed to learning about it and assisting the potential client. The client must be aware that you must include this information in the representation agreement. Generally, however, and to avoid any claims of ineffective assistance from counsel, it is best to stay in your known and familiar practice area.

In addition, the scope of representation should include matters in which you will not participate. For example, your firm may represent a health care professional in a disciplinary matter up to a certain point in the proceeding, including the agency's decision. However, under this representation agreement, you will not be obligated to handle an appeal should the client wish to appeal the agency's decision. As another example, in a criminal matter, the conclusion of representation may occur after a plea is entered or after sentencing. Therefore, the scope of representation should specifically state when the representation will be concluded.

In some instances, while representing clients, a new matter may arise. For example, when representing a disciplinary defense matter related to complaint #1, the client receives a second complaint. If this happens, consider amending the representation agreement to include the additional complaint. Alternatively, the representation agreement may include a provision that the scope will include the initial complaint, as well as any others that may be filed during the pendency of the initial matter.

Consider pro bono matters. Your State Bar may mandate a certain number of pro bono hours. Also, consider referring matters to other attorneys if you cannot offer effective assistance. Be acquainted with practitioners who specialize in areas of law that you lack experience or knowledge, and in so doing, develop a referral network. Typically, when you refer to the family law attorney or the criminal defense attorney, the favor is returned if those attorneys are unfamiliar with your specialized area of practice.

CHAPTER 5

Billing and Record-Keeping

Conswella M. Byrd, RN, BSN, JD

DISCLOSURE

THE AUTHOR HAS NO FINANCIAL INTERESTS OR RELATIONSHIPS WITH ANY OF THE PRODUCTS OR PROGRAMS SUGGESTED IN THIS CHAPTER, NOR DO THEY ENDORSE THEM.

DISCLAIMER

WHILE THIS CHAPTER GUIDEBOOK OFFERS GUIDANCE ON SOLO PRACTICE, IT SHOULD NOT BE CONSTRUED AS LEGAL ADVICE.

LETTERS OF ENGAGEMENT

An engagement letter is an agreement that describes the services that a firm is offering to provide to a client. The letter is essentially an abbreviated contract that defines the services to be performed and the amount of compensation to be paid.

- Authorized representatives of both parties must sign an engagement letter for it to be considered a legally binding arrangement. Since this letter is treated as a contract, it should address the obligations of both parties, including the following issues: the exact services to be provided, including any due dates, performance criteria, the exact amount and timing of payments to be made by the client, any warranties of performance, and how either party can terminate the contract.

FEE AGREEMENTS

- One of the keys to a successful attorney-client relationship is the client having confidence in the attorney's advice and in the amount of the attorney fees incurred in rendering that advice. Aligning your fees and income with your clients' goals will enable your law practice to deliver value effectively and efficiently.

- It is important to note that the attorney-client relationship can begin without an official fee agreement between the attorney and client. Rather, because the attorney-client relationship is contractual in nature, it begins when an attorney agrees to render professional services for a client. This agreement may be specifically outlined or implied from the conduct of the parties. Your state Bar may have specific requirements for fee agreements.

PRO BONO

The term "pro bono" is derived from the Latin phrase "pro bono publico," meaning "for the public good." The provider of a pro bono service may generally do so only to a party that cannot afford their services, or, in their discretion, to anyone. In doing so, the provider is perceived to impart a benefit for the greater good, rather than for the typical profit motive.

FLAT FEE

Flat fees, also known as fixed fees, are prearranged total fees that are paid upfront before you complete work for a particular legal matter. For example, for standard DUI cases, drafting wills, bankruptcy, or other form-based matters, flat fees may be attractive for both the client and the attorney because these sorts of matters usually have no surprises and no fee collection hassles.

HOURLY FEES

- Hourly billing is what most people associate with attorney fees. However, this method of law firm pricing and fees is becoming antiquated and is no longer as client-friendly. As technology progresses, clients expect greater transparency and predictability in pricing from their attorneys. With hourly billing, clients may feel anxious about their legal bill because they don't know what the final number will be. They could feel like the value they receive from your services is less than what they paid. Worse, your clients may view hourly rates as an incentive for you to be inefficient and take your time with their matters, causing distrust in your relationship with clients. Clients don't really want to pay for your time; they want to pay for the help and value you provide them.

- Hourly rates aren't the best option for attorneys either. Hourly rates don't allow your time to scale and limit your time for other matters and opportunities. Charging an hourly rate means your earnings will always be capped by the amount of time you work. If you still want or need to charge by the hour, your rate should be based on a combination of the following factors: your expertise in the subject, competitive rates in your jurisdiction, the type of case and matter, and the type of client.

STAGED FLAT FEES

Efforts that can be broken down into discrete stages might be suitable for a staged flat fee. Thus, if there are four stages to a matter, you can set a flat fee for each stage. If you do not need to complete certain stages, then the client does not pay you for those stages. This fee structure is a useful hybrid between billing by the hour and a pure flat fee, as it provides the client with greater cost certainty than the billable hour while avoiding a single flat fee payment that reflects a higher anticipated fee than the actual time worked.

RETAINER

Another derivative of the hourly rate is retainers, which are a lump sum that clients pay up front, from which you deduct your hourly fees.

Retainers are also used to secure your availability as an attorney. When implementing retainer agreements, you will consider the work that needs to be completed or the opportunities lost because of the commitment to your availability.

CONTINGENCY

Contingency fees allow you to take a certain percentage of the monetary settlement or damages your client receives as your attorney's fee. You should check your state Bar rules regarding the percentages allowed and requirements.

> ABA Model Rule 1.5(d) prohibits using contingency fees for divorce cases where the fee is contingent on securing the divorce or getting an amount of alimony, support, or property, and criminal cases. You should check with your state Bar ethics rules to ensure that certain cases can be charged on a contingency basis.

INSURED

Group legal services resemble group health insurance. For an annual fee, members are entitled to low-cost or free consultations with an attorney. The attorney receives client referrals from the legal insurance company, which will pay the attorney, but often for a reduced fee. Several forms of group legal services exist, ranging from employee-provided benefits to commercially marketed plans. These vary in scope, price, and availability.

- Federal and state regulations govern plans for group legal services. Employer-provided plans fall under the Employee Retirement Income Security Act (ERISA) (29 U.S.C.A. § 1001 et seq.). Enacted in 1974, ERISA protects employees' Pension rights and imposes strict fiduciary requirements on their group legal services. Other types of plans are subject to state laws, which generally impose light regulation and follow the legal profession's

Model Rules of Professional Conduct in such areas as ethics and attorney-client Privilege.

- For further information, please see Chapter 8.

INVOICING, PAYMENT, COLLECTION

Once you perform the required work, your billing process begins with the invoice. Your invoice is one of the many ways you communicate the value of your services to your clients. Your invoices should be clear and concise, allowing your clients to read them easily. After all, when they know what they're being billed for, they're more likely to pay.

ELEMENTS OF YOUR INVOICE

Using billing or practice management software will allow you to create uniform invoices with built-in templates. Your invoice template should include a few key elements:

- **Service description**: This includes a description of the legal services that you provided, as detailed as possible. Simply stating "legal services" with the total number of hours spent isn't enough. You should describe each service you provide.
- **Contact information**: Include your client's name, address, and phone number. Do the same for your firm.
- **Dates**: Include the invoice date and the expected payment date.
- **Invoice number**: This helps you keep track of each invoice you send, and your clients keep track of which ones they've paid.
- **Payment methods**: Describe the payment methods you accept, such as cash, check, credit card, etc. Accepting multiple payment methods gives your clients more flexibility, increasing the likelihood of on-time payments. Many billing programs allow you to send invoices electronically and include a link to your credit card payment method.
- **Total**: Include the total service cost on your invoice.

MONITORING PAYMENTS

Your accounts receivable represent the money owed to your firm by your debtors and your clients. You should monitor your accounts receivable regularly. If you use billing or bookkeeping software, you should have access to an accounts receivable report showing past-due accounts.

- Invoices typically go to collections after a certain amount of time passes without payment. It is typical for any organization to wait at least a month or so before beginning the collections process. The Consumer Protection Act 68 of 2008 states that "A consumer must receive a quote or breakdown of his/her financial obligations before agreeing." Therefore, penalties for late payments must be covered in any agreement with your client. Make sure the section is easy to read and clearly written. Keep your terms brief and straightforward. Check your state Bar Rules.

FEE DISPUTES

California Rule of Professional Responsibility 3.501 entitles a client to arbitration of a dispute regarding an attorney's fees for legal services. If initiated by a client, fee arbitration is mandatory for an attorney. Fee arbitration is voluntary for a client unless the parties have agreed in writing to submit their fee disputes to mandatory fee arbitration. Check your state Bar Rules for the governing law in your state.

- For more information, refer to Chapter 7.

BILLING STATEMENTS: PRINT AND EMAIL

Legal billing software ensures lawyers and law firms collect payment for their time and effort. These billing systems are optimized for the law profession and incorporate features like time tracking, invoicing, and some accounting capabilities. Legal billing software often integrates with case management systems and larger accounting platforms to maintain a holistic view of the attorneys and staff contributing to specific cases and where a firm has yet to reconcile outstanding debts.

RATE-SETTING: BY MATTER OR CLIENT

Setting your pricing requires that you understand the value of your work. Value will mean different things to different clients. One client will find emotional value in the relief you can give them, while another will get financial value through a contract you help negotiate for their business. You can initially communicate value to clients through your marketing campaigns and during your client consultation. Still, ideally, those should be a means to attract your ideal clients, so you don't have to defend the pricing for your services. In setting your rate, you should consider: your expertise in the subject, competitive rates in your jurisdiction, the type of case and matter, and the type of client.

TRANSACTION RECORDS

Client trust accounting is a process that demonstrates to your clients that you know how much of the money in your account belongs to each client. Failure to fulfill this responsibility can result in personal financial liability, fee disputes, loss of clients, and public discipline. Check your State Bar Rules for the governing law in your state.

CLIENT MATTER NOTES

- As a registered nurse, you wrote nurse's notes regarding your patient's progress, condition, etc. Nurse's notes are included in the patient's medical record and are discoverable.
- An attorney's client matter notes are kept in the client's file and generally include thoughts, observations, impressions, or questions related to the client. These notes may also contain internal office management memoranda, such as personnel assignments or conflict of interest

checks, facts related to the client's case, and items reasonably necessary to a client's representation.

- The State Bars Rules of Professional Conduct define the client file documents that must be returned to the client and are discoverable, as opposed to those that a lawyer may ethically retain and are not required to return. Generally, the client is entitled to all documents provided initially by the client, and all documents filed, served, or sent by the lawyer to others.

STATE, FEDERAL AND PROFESSIONAL ETHICS RULES

The inclusion of the numerous state, federal, and professional ethics rules regarding billing and record-keeping is beyond the scope of this chapter. Check your State Bar Rules for the governing law in your state.

ACCOUNTING AND BOOKKEEPING FOR RECONCILIATIONS

Account reconciliation is the process of comparing internal financial records against monthly statements from external sources, such as banks, credit card companies, or other financial institutions, to identify any discrepancies. Knowing how to reconcile your accounts accurately is essential for the financial health of your law practice, as it helps detect errors, discrepancies, or fraud. When you use accounting software to reconcile accounts, the software does most of the work for you, saving you a good deal of time.

REFERENCES

1. lawyerist.com
2. https://alegaldictionary.com
3. https://legal-dictionary.thefreedictionary.com.
4. http://www.calbar.ca.gov

5. MCLE Self Study, February 2012 | Mrs. Smith called; she wants her file …By Wendy L. Patrick, 2020 The State Bar of California, https://apps.calbar.ca.gov/mcleselfstudy/mcle_home.aspx?testid=58
6. Wisconsin Lawyer: Ethics: What Comprises a Client File?, Dean R. Dietrich, 2020 State Bar of Wisconsin.

CHAPTER 6

Office Management

Janet E. Michael, BSN, MSN, JD

BAR ASSOCIATION LICENSURE REQUIREMENTS

The website of each state's bar association (licensing board) contains a wealth of information to assist solo practitioners. Additionally, most bar associations have staff willing to provide guidance and clarify bar rules. Some may even have designated call-in times for attorneys with ethical questions or concerns.

CONTINUING LEGAL EDUCATION (CLE) REQUIREMENTS

Many states have specific requirements regarding the type and number of CLE hours required to renew one's license. For example, attorneys may be required to complete 12 hours of CLE credit each calendar year (or fiscal year) to renew their bar license. There is also generally a requirement that a certain number of the CLE hours (six or more) must be live hours. These may be in-person education or virtual CLE participation by Zoom, WebEx, or other visual platforms. The remaining CLE hours can be self-study.

Additionally, many states require that each attorney complete one or two hours of ethics and professional responsibility CLEs. There may also be a requirement to complete other specific subject matter, such as training in current topics. An example would be CLE discussing harassment and discrimination awareness.

Some CLE courses are offered by providers pre-authorized by your state bar to provide CLE educational offerings. Other providers have not sought such pre-authorization. When you take a course from a provider who has not been pre-approved, you must file an application for approval of CLE credit. A fee is often required to process the application.

PRO BONO REQUIREMENTS

You can find the basis for the rendering of pro bono legal services in the American Bar Association (ABA Model Rule 6.1), which establishes a professional responsibility for every lawyer to provide legal services to those unable to pay. The ABA recommends that all lawyers should strive to provide at least 50 hours of pro bono legal services per year.

Regardless of the ABA Model Rule, the requirements relating to pro bono services vary significantly from state to state. For example, New York is the only state that requires pro bono services to be rendered to qualify for bar admission in that state. Nine (9) states require attorneys to report their pro bono hours at license renewal. Those states are Florida, Hawaii, Illinois, Indiana, Maryland, Mississippi, Nevada, New Mexico, and New York. Thirteen (13) states have rules that suggest voluntary reporting of pro bono hours. They are Arizona, Connecticut, Georgia, Kentucky, Louisiana, Montana, North Carolina, Ohio, Oregon, Tennessee, Texas, Virginia, and Washington. No other states currently have any pro bono requirements.

TRUST ACCOUNTS REQUIRED

A trust account retains client funds until the attorney has earned or expended them on behalf of the client. Currently, all states, the District of Columbia, and the U.S. Virgin Islands operate Interest on Lawyer Trust Accounts (IOLTA) as a method of raising funds for charitable purposes by utilizing the interest earned from IOLTA accounts to provide legal services to those who cannot afford them. Not only are IOLTA accounts available in all states, but they must also be listed on most bar renewals.

You can set up a properly titled IOLTA account at your bank. Once the account is set up, you should always maintain a double record of transactions, and ensure that the account is always reconciled. [Also, see Chapter 1.]

CODE OF ETHICS

The ABA Model Code of Judicial Conduct was adopted in 1972 and recently revised in 2010. It comprises a Preamble, a Terminology section, and four Canons, each accompanied by comments. Prior editions of the Model Code were titled the ABA Canons of Judicial Conduct. The text of the Model Code is usually included in most sources that have the Model Rules and Code for lawyers. The current Model Code is available online, and it shows comparisons to prior editions.

The Model Code of Judicial Conduct is reprinted in the ABA's annual publication Model Rules of Professional Conduct (Reserve KF306. A74816). An annotated version of the most recent judicial code is also available (KF8779.A96 2011).

Like the rules for lawyers, each state adopts its own rules for judicial conduct, and most are based on this ABA model. State judicial conduct codes are generally reproduced in state court rules publications and databases. If you have an ethical question, many of the state bar licensing boards offer call-in times during you can ask an ethical question. There are attorneys in most states who have earned a reputation for their insight on ethical questions, and most of them are happy to share their insights. If you have an ethical dilemma, contact trusted resources to ask the questions needed to find the best answer.

CALENDER SYSTEM

Today, a variety of calendar systems are available. When choosing the one that is best for you, you need to look for something tailored for an attorney in solo practice that will meet your specific needs.

Before looking at available calendar systems, consider your needs. Decide whether you will be the sole user of the system or if you will have another person also enter information and access the calendar. List all the ways that you want to use your calendar system. What would you like the calendar system to track for you?

Prioritize the features that are most important for you in a calendar system. For example, do you want to be able to integrate your calendar into your computer and on your smartphone? Do you want an alarm system to remind you of important meetings or tasks to be completed? (Yes, you do!) Do you want a scheduling feature to make client appointments easy to document and track?

Once you have decided what you need, start looking at calendar systems. Read reviews of calendar systems and talk to other attorneys to determine what they consider the most user-friendly system. Check with the professional organizations you belong to and see if they offer a discount on a specific type of system. If you find a calendar system that has most of the features you like, request a free trial to make sure that it actually meets your needs and is the best system for your day-to-day use. Take this trial period to explore the system as much as your imagination allows. Ease of use is essential, allowing you to regularly use the system and utilize it optimally.

ANSWERING SERVICE/MESSAGING SYSTEM

A solo practitioner without a full or even a part-time employee may or may not want to invest in the monthly charges associated with a formal answering service/messaging system. In reality, it may be sufficient to have a reliable voicemail service that allows you to access it remotely and forward calls to other locations.

Use the same process suggested above to choose a calendar system and select an answering/message service that will meet your needs and prevent unnecessary expenses. The most important thing for any attorney to do regarding phone messages is to return each and every call promptly, within 24 hours or sooner.

RECORDS MANAGEMENT AND STORAGE

Your open files should be kept in fireproof file cabinets as noted in Chapter 2.

How you organize your files is a matter of personal choice. Some attorneys like to arrange files strictly in alphabetical order, and others arrange them in terms of the type of case involved (such as the type of administrative board). Maintain the records in a user-friendly manner that enables you to access the needed files easily and effectively. It is best practice to keep a list of all clients and the exact file location of each of their files as a cross-reference.

In general, you should keep all client records for seven (7) years from the time of closing the file. These may be kept in paper form or in a scanned format on a thumb drive, external hard drive, or in "the cloud." Remember that the mode of storage and how the file is to be handled upon storage should be noted as part of your representation agreement.

Off-site storage is well-suited for storing files in paper form. Off-site storage units should require an entrance code to enter and then allow for a securely locked and fireproof storage unit. All boxes should be clearly marked by year, box number, and any other desired identifiers. Remember to complete and update a list of the location of each stored file so that it can easily be accessed when necessary.

EMPLOYEES OR INDEPENDENT CONTRACTORS

A sole practitioner may or may not want full-time or part-time employees. It depends on what tasks you wish to delegate to an employee. For example, to save time during a busy workday, you may have someone run errands or pick up mail at a post office box. If you have print, copy, and scanning work that needs to be done, you may engage a service with expertise and staff to do those tasks, thus saving you significant amounts of time. An independent contractor can give you flexibility for cost savings. Yet that approach may not be possible in every state. In some states, non-lawyers who require direct supervision must be treated as employees. California has stringent guidelines for determining an individual's status. Know your state's employment rules.

Of course, whenever you hire someone to work in your office or contractually do work for you, you must ensure the confidentiality of client-related documents and other information.

You may also need occasional help writing a brief or preparing for a complicated hearing. In such an instance, you may want to hire another attorney to help with the legal research needed for an individual case or organizing documents for the actual hearing. Hiring a nurse attorney who has just graduated from law school can be very helpful. When hiring someone to conduct legal research, ensure they have a competent level of familiarity with the type and version of the software used.

Know the workload you want to delegate. If you have a full- or part-time employee, it is important to plan enough work to keep them busy. This may be difficult given the technological advances that make it challenging for even large law firms to keep employees busy assisting just one attorney on a day-to-day basis.

EMPLOYEE AND SELF-BENEFITS

When hiring full-time or part-time employees, it is often essential to offer a comprehensive benefits package. The most important benefits to provide are paid vacation time and holidays, as well as health and dental insurance. Other benefits are generally negotiable and dependent on the individual employee's needs.

Sometimes, bar associations and other professional associations have insurance groups through which you can obtain health insurance for your employees and yourself. At other times, you may need to set up your own group plan.

If you, as a solo attorney, do not have employees and a spouse who can provide insurance benefits through their place of employment, you need to make plans to ensure that you have the needed health and dental insurance. Additionally, seriously consider purchasing life insurance, long-term and short-term disability insurance, business interruption insurance, property insurance, liability insurance (including an umbrella policy), malpractice insurance, and potentially cyber-insurance. See Chapter 1 for more information about suggested insurance coverage.

CHAPTER 7

Client Management

Edie Brous, RN, BSN, MS, MPH, JD

DISCLOSURE

THE AUTHOR HAS NO FINANCIAL INTERESTS OR RELATIONSHIPS WITH ANY OF THE PRODUCTS OR PROGRAMS SUGGESTED IN THIS CHAPTER, NOR DO THEY ENDORSE THEM.

DISCLAIMER

WHILE THIS CHAPTER GUIDEBOOK OFFERS GUIDANCE ON SOLO PRACTICE, IT SHOULD NOT BE CONSTRUED AS LEGAL ADVICE.

CLIENT SELECTION

Chapter 4 discussed the logistics of client selection and the scopes of representation. This chapter will discuss additional selection concerns and considerations of professional conduct rules, communications, and fee disputes.

From a humanistic or economic standpoint, you might be tempted to represent every potential client requesting your services. Avoid that temptation. In the interests of risk management and providing the best service to people with legal needs, you should carefully screen and select your clients. You can accept some potential clients, decline others, and refer some to other legal practitioners. Whether to accept, decline, or refer a client is a business decision that requires careful consideration of multiple factors.

Poor client selection will increase your stress level, drain your resources, and expose you to liability. Poor client selection can also result in the need to terminate a relationship, which presents its own set of problems. Using a large search engine, such as Google, to screen potential clients is a suggested standard intake practice. Internet searches can provide red flag warnings, such as criminal histories or prior litigation. Taking a look at a potential client's use of social media can also prevent problems by alerting you to any worrisome internet presence early on. Additionally, if the client is a licensed professional, conducting a license verification can provide you with information that the client might not have shared with you.

CONSIDERATIONS IN CLIENT SELECTIONS

- Is this the kind of case with which you have the required expertise? Can you skillfully handle the matter?
- You will be able to manage some cases alone. You can manage other cases with an experienced colleague who can mentor you through the matter. Be honest with yourself. You won't be able to provide competent counsel in an area with which you have no experience. "Dabbling" is not good practice. Some cases might be within your expertise, but they will be too time-consuming for a solo or require resources better met in a larger firm.
- Will the client be able to pay you?
- Unless you willingly choose to provide pro bono services or accept an assignment of benefits from an insurance company, you should not accept clients who cannot afford your fee. You will spend too much time pursuing them to make payments, and this will set you up for fee disputes. Avoid providing services for which you will not be compensated. Discuss your fees and provide the potential client with a realistic amount for which they will be responsible. Don't agree to take the case until you have received the fee and a signed letter of engagement.
- Is the potential client a family member, colleague, or personal friend?
- This should be an alarm bell. It is potentially risky to represent someone with whom you have a personal relationship. It can also violate

ethical requirements in some conditions. If you do take on such a matter, be particularly careful to treat the case as you would any other in terms of representation limits, written communications, and file management.

- Is the potential client someone with whom you can work?
- You can't have an effective attorney-client relationship with all people. Potential clients who are not forthcoming, are unable to hear realistic assessments of their situation, have goals that are irreconcilable with your advice, have unrealizable expectations, expect you to accomplish the impossible, have misunderstandings about an attorney's role, or suggest that you act unethically or illegally, should set off loud alarm bells. Other potential clients might have none of these issues, but do not "feel right" to you. Trust your gut. Some clients will do better with one of your colleagues than with you. Here is a tip that can save you headaches: Do not accept a client who has had multiple previous attorneys or disparages previous counsel.
- Has the potential client waited until the last minute to seek counsel?
- If there are time-sensitive issues, the client can expect you to respond rapidly, even though good practice would typically require more time. Ask the client why they are seeking counsel now instead of earlier. Do not accept the case if you don't have the time to meet any deadlines. You can tell the client that you can only provide responsible legal assistance if they can obtain an extension on the due date.
- Will accepting this client present a conflict of interest?
- If there is any chance that your representation of this client will be compromised by your representation of another client (current or former) or your own interests, you should decline representation or refer the client to another qualified attorney.

When declining a case, send a declination letter. Remind the client of any statute of limitations or other deadline concerns and the need to contact another attorney. In this letter, state that the meeting did not create an attorney-client relationship.

In addition to the above considerations, familiarize your jurisdiction's rules of professional conduct, as they might specifically address client selection. New York's Rule 1.16, for example, says:

> *Declining or Terminating Representation*
>
> *(a) A lawyer shall not accept employment on behalf of a person if the lawyer knows or reasonably should know that such person wishes to:*
>
> *(1) bring a legal action, conduct a defense, or assert a position in a matter, or otherwise have steps taken for such person, merely for the purpose of harassing or maliciously injuring any person; or*
>
> *(2) present a claim or defense in a matter that is not warranted under existing law, unless it can be supported by a good faith argument for an extension, modification, or reversal of existing law.*
>
> *(b) Except as stated in paragraph (d), a lawyer shall withdraw from the representation of a client when:*
>
> *(1) the lawyer knows or reasonably should know that the representation will result in a violation of these* Rules *or of law;*
>
> *(2) the lawyer's physical or mental condition materially impairs the lawyer's ability to represent the client;*
>
> *(3) the lawyer is discharged; or*
>
> *(4) the lawyer knows or reasonably should know that the client is bringing legal action, conducting the defense, or asserting a position in the matter, or is otherwise having steps taken, merely for the purpose of harassing or maliciously injuring any person.*
>
> *(c) Except as stated in paragraph (d), a lawyer may withdraw from representing a client when:*
>
> *(1) withdrawal can be accomplished without material adverse effect on the interests of the client;*

(2) the client persists in a course of action involving the lawyer's services that the lawyer reasonably believes is criminal or fraudulent;

(3) the client has used the lawyer's services to perpetrate a crime or fraud;

(4) the client insists upon taking action with which the lawyer has a fundamental disagreement;

(5) the client deliberately disregards an agreement or obligation to the lawyer as to expenses or fees;

(6) the client insists upon presenting a claim or defense that is not warranted under existing law and cannot be supported by good faith argument for an extension, modification, or reversal of existing law;

(7) the client fails to cooperate in the representation or otherwise renders the representation unreasonably difficult for the lawyer to carry out employment effectively;

(8) the lawyer's inability to work with co-counsel indicates that the best interest of the client likely will be served by withdrawal;

(9) the lawyer's mental or physical condition renders it difficult for the lawyer to carry out the representation effectively;

(10) the client knowingly and freely assents to termination of the employment;

(11) withdrawal is permitted under Rule *1.13(c) or other law;*

(12) the lawyer believes in good faith, in a matter pending before a tribunal, that the tribunal will find the existence of other good cause for withdrawal; or

(13) the client insists that the lawyer pursue a course of conduct which is illegal or prohibited under these Rules.

(d) If permission for withdrawal from employment is required by the rules of a tribunal, a lawyer shall not withdraw from employment in a matter before that tribunal without its permission. When ordered to do so by a tribunal, a lawyer shall continue representation notwithstanding good cause for terminating the representation.

(e) Even when withdrawal is otherwise permitted or required, upon termination of representation, a lawyer shall take steps, to the extent reasonably practicable, to

avoid foreseeable prejudice to the rights of the client, including giving reasonable notice to the client, allowing time for employment of other counsel, delivering to the client all papers and property to which the client is entitled, promptly refunding any part of a fee paid in advance that has not been earned and complying with applicable laws and rules.

CLIENT COMMUNICATION

Written communications are essential for your own protection and for the client's benefit. Many clients have difficulty processing and retaining information. Some written communications that can be helpful include:

- Engagement agreements that specifically outline the scope and limits of your representation
- Periodic billing statements that specifically describe the work being done
- Declination letters
- Status reports
- New client materials and instructions upon being engaged
- A statement of client rights and responsibilities
- Settlement discussions detailing the risks, benefits, alternatives, and costs of settling or attending a hearing/going to trial
- Disengagement/withdrawal letters
- Termination of service/closing letters that clearly advise the client that the attorney/client relationship is being terminated and your legal representation is complete.

Providing written instructions and reviews of discussions, strategies, etc., will give the client something tangible to review and provide documentation for you should there be any later claims that the client did not understand or agree to something. Email correspondence provides a written record of communications. Earlier chapters address the critical importance of security when communicating electronically, as well as the use of client portals in practice management systems. The client should agree to electronic communication in writing and be advised not to send emails to you from an employer setting or use unprotected servers. You can do this in the initial letter of engagement. Sample language might be:

> *The client approves the use of electronic communications and storage, such as credit card transactions, cloud services, photocopiers, email, eFax, and fax, and the use of a client portal, and agrees to send such communications from protected devices and servers, avoiding any monitored or shared devices and servers.*

Telephone conferences or virtual meetings should be memorialized in writing. For example, "as we discussed on the telephone/in the video conference this morning," followed by references to topics discussed on calls. Add letters and real-time notes to your own files and itemize these meetings in your billing statements.

Your document retention and destruction practices should be consistent with professional conduct standards and clearly communicated to clients in an engagement letter. Sample language might be:

> *When the Attorney's services conclude, all unpaid charges shall become immediately due and payable. After Attorney's services conclude, Attorney will, at Client's request, turn over to Client all Client's file, along with any Client funds or property in Attorney's possession. The Attorney will maintain all data and file materials for seven years from the conclusion of the representation.*

FEE DISPUTES

Conflicts over billing pose liability issues for the solo practitioner. Your written communications must clearly explain your fee schedules, billing practices, payment expectations, and how disputes will be handled. Client portals for evergreen reports can provide access for the client and documentation for you, as can frequent billing statements or invoices. It is essential to know if your state has specific provisions for resolving fee disputes.

Some jurisdictions mandate participation in formal fee dispute resolution arbitration/mediation programs. Upon engagement, clients need to be notified of their right to participate in these programs, and the state can specify how much notice is required before filing a claim for fees. It can help to routinely give the state's fee dispute information to the client at the beginning of the representation and have a record of that.

In some cases, it may be better to remain unpaid rather than to pursue collections, as this frequently results in counterclaims or complaints to bar associations and reports to malpractice insurance companies. Pursuing fees during representation can also create conflicts of interest. During a dispute, put all earned and undisputed funds into your operating account and all disputed funds in trust until the matter is resolved.

COMMUNICATION SKILLS

Many, if not most, clients are stressed or even traumatized by their legal problems. Their contact with you may be the first time they have ever needed an attorney, and it can be difficult to obtain a coherent chronology of events from them. It can be challenging for them to understand or follow your directions. It is important to distinguish between willful non-adherence and traumatized behavior. Very anxious clients require additional support, repeated explanations, and frequent communication. You might need to refer some clients to trauma counselors for support if their anxiety compromises your ability to represent them effectively. Willful non-adherence might be a reason you consider terminating the representation.

Some clients have distorted views of attorney advocacy. Television and cinema characterizations of lawyers frequently depict them as aggressive "pit bulls," and clients might think that is the way they should conduct themselves with their adversaries. This expectation can be intensified when the client feels resentful about their situation or is seeking revenge. Take the time to explain that aggressive approaches can be counterproductive, and although you understand their feelings, your goal is to obtain the best outcome for them, not to win an argument. Clarify the client's goals. For example, you may ask, "Do you want to be **right**, or do you want to be **effective**?" It can be helpful for some clients to obtain a consultation and second opinion from other counsel, so they feel assured that you are taking the right approach.

Some clients will require limit-setting for your own well-being and to prevent disruption to your practice. Anxiety can reduce a client's impulse control and ability to understand what is and is not an emergency. Set clear boundaries so clients know when and how you are available. Firmly establish and maintain the nature of your relationship as being limited to managing a specific legal issue, not other matters or personal issues. It is not advisable to share your home or cell phone numbers, or private email addresses that you use for personal matters, with clients. It is also not good practice to connect with clients on social media.

Question batching can be helpful for needy clients. Establish a regular speaking schedule and have the client save all questions for that scheduled time. Define what is and what is not urgent. Solo practitioners can fall into the 24-hour availability/on-call trap. Clients must understand that you are only available to them during your business hours. Do not respond to voice messages or emails on weekends, evenings, vacations, or holidays. If you will be out of the office for a period of time, set up an automatic email response that provides the dates you will be out of the office and only respond to actual emergencies.

Discourage clients from texting you or communicating with you. Text messages are disruptive and not a secure method of communication. Anxious people sometimes send attorneys unsolicited documents and detailed descriptions of their problems. Respond by telling them that, unless or until an established attorney-client relationship is established, they should not discuss the details of their matters or send documents to anyone.

You might need to repeatedly explain that there will not be immediate answers or resolution, and that holding patterns and waiting periods are normal. Addressing the process and time frames in a client engagement letter can help manage expectations. Frequent education on how the legal system operates can reassure clients that you are still involved in their representation even when nothing seems to be happening. Clients can directly contact adversaries when they are impatient or anxious. Make it clear at the outset that all communication with adversaries must be through you. Such direct contact can compromise their case and your ability to advocate for them effectively. Clearly outline communication expectations in the engagement agreement, the new client instructions and materials, and in all other written communications with the client. Advise your clients that their direct communication with adversaries can be grounds for you to withdraw from representation.

Clients with substance use disorders, mental health issues, or personality disorders can be demanding to represent. Some clients can become disrespectful or abusive. Some can disregard your advice. Some can be deceitful. Clients with a history of successful legal cases may be perceived as competitive or manipulative. Unlike a larger firm, where these clients can be reassigned to a different attorney, in these circumstances, solo practitioners might need to terminate the attorney-client relationship. Do so carefully. Know what professional conduct rules and procedures are in place in your state(s) regarding withdrawal, and make sure the client will not be prejudiced or compromised by inadequate time to retain other counsel. Follow any court requirements for permission to withdraw.

DISCHARGE AND WITHDRAWAL

Discharge and withdrawal should be addressed in the letter of engagement. Sample language can include:

> *The client may discharge the Attorney at any time. The attorney may withdraw from representing a Client for good cause. Good cause includes, but is not limited to, breach of any material terms of this Contract, intentional misrepresentation or deception by Client, Client's failure to cooperate with Attorney, or failure to follow Attorney's advice on a material matter, to pay bills on time, client's direct communication with adverse parties, or any other fact or circumstance that would render Attorney's continuing representation unlawful or unethical.*

Memorialize the termination or withdrawal process in writing. The client should be advised of pending deadlines, resources for obtaining new counsel, and the ability to have their file returned or sent to new counsel. Return any unused funds or trust account property and provide a detailed and itemized final billing statement that reflects the work you have performed.

Conversations a lawyer considers informal, off the cuff, or theoretical can be construed by others as having established an attorney-client relationship. Be clear in your email signature, as a first slide in any presentations, as an initial statement in publications, and in these "curbside consults" that you are not creating this relationship, providing legal counsel, or advising on a matter.

Cautious client selection and properly maintained professional boundaries are critical aspects of solo practice. Clarifying practice boundaries can avoid complications by ensuring careful adherence to these principles.

CHAPTER 8

Career Opportunities for Nurse Attorneys

INTRODUCTION

Eileen Talamonte, RN, BSN, JD

DISCLOSURE

THE AUTHOR HAS NO FINANCIAL INTERESTS OR RELATIONSHIPS WITH ANY OF THE PRODUCTS OR PROGRAMS SUGGESTED IN THIS CHAPTER, NOR DO THEY ENDORSE THEM.

DISCLAIMER

WHILE THIS CHAPTER GUIDEBOOK OFFERS GUIDANCE ON SOLO PRACTICE, IT SHOULD NOT BE CONSTRUED AS LEGAL ADVICE.

So, you've obtained dual degrees and licenses in nursing and law, and you want to open a solo practice. Congratulations! Now what? Initially, this may have seemed like a simple question. Perhaps you thought this chapter would set before you a definitive and limited list of options for you to choose from as you plan your solo law practice. However, the reality of having dual licensure in nursing and law is that your options are limited only by your own unique qualifications, imagination, instincts, educational pursuits, and, for some, entrepreneurial spirit.

Throughout your professional life as a nurse attorney, you will not necessarily need to limit yourself to one "career" type. Instead, you may decide to evolve and transition to and from numerous and possibly overlapping roles on your personal journey as a nurse attorney. In short, this subject could fill an entire book, let alone a chapter.

It is important to note that this chapter deliberately focuses on career paths that generally require a nurse to be an attorney licensed by a state bar and, therefore, possessing the potential to develop a solo law practice. However, we would be remiss if we did not acknowledge the wide range of additional career options available for nurses with law degrees who may or may not be licensed to practice. Many of these individuals have extremely fulfilling careers, making outstanding contributions in both the public and private sectors as educators, entrepreneurs, nurse coaches, authors, consultants, risk managers, state and federal employees, political and public policy advocates, and in various corporate settings. A complete list of possibilities could be the basis for another chapter or book.

Nurses are advocates by nature. It is the essence of our calling. We strive to ensure that all patient rights are respected and protected. We continually develop and utilize our critical thinking and problem-solving skills to provide the highest level of care to patients under a myriad of often tough and unanticipated circumstances. Perhaps, most importantly, we are called to approach every patient the same, without judgment, as a unique individual worthy of our care, regardless of race, gender, or economics.

Whichever path you choose in your law practice, the nursing skills you developed through your nursing experiences, will be at the core of what makes you extraordinarily well-suited to represent the needs and interests of clients in many areas of the law, such as criminal law, disciplinary and licensure defense for all licensed health care providers, elder law, employment law, estate planning, family law, health care law, immigration law, litigation (plaintiff and defense), and mediation/arbitration.

We cannot discuss all these specialties in this chapter, but we hope to give you a well-chosen sample to help you narrow down your options and choose a path suited to your unique strengths and interests.

***

ADVANCED NURSING PRACTICE

Melanie Balestra, RN, PNP, MN, JD

DISCLOSURE

THE AUTHOR HAS NO FINANCIAL INTERESTS OR RELATIONSHIPS WITH ANY OF THE PRODUCTS OR PROGRAMS SUGGESTED IN THIS CHAPTER, NOR DO THEY ENDORSE THEM.

DISCLAIMER

WHILE THIS CHAPTER GUIDEBOOK OFFERS GUIDANCE ON SOLO PRACTICE, IT SHOULD NOT BE CONSTRUED AS LEGAL ADVICE.

There are more than 385,000 nurse practitioners (NPs) licensed in the United States. It is one of the fastest-growing professions in the US. Thirty-four states now have full practice authority, which means NPs can practice without any supervision by physicians. This presents an incredible opportunity in a variety of areas.

One first thinks of malpractice claims or disciplinary actions. The most recent CNA/NSO claims study showed that the average cost of an NP malpractice claim is $332,137, an increase of over 10.5% from 2012 to 2017. The number of license defense claims has increased by 80% since the last report. Licensure defending costs have increased by 19.5%. The increase in malpractice included diagnosis errors, medication prescribing issues, and problems with treatment and care. As NPs become more visible as health care providers, it is understandable how malpractice and disciplinary claims will increase. NPs must have their own malpractice/disciplinary insurance coverage. Nurse attorneys have the knowledge and experience to represent NPs better than most attorneys. TAANA's association with NSO/HPSO encourages members to be on the NSO/HPSO referral list.

There are many NP state, national, and specialty organizations. These organizations all need legal advice and representation. Most organizations also have yearly conferences. Submitting an abstract for a presentation on liability and/or scope of practice issues can help the nurse attorney gain recognition from the associations and their members. Also, many of these organizations have journals or newsletters. Writing journal articles and/or a news column on nurse practitioner issues will get the nurse attorney's name recognized. When an NP problem arises, the nurse attorney's name will be common and most accessible to the NP.

With more and more states recognizing full practice authority, NPs are starting their own practices or becoming entrepreneurs in other businesses, such as coaching. NPs need legal advice to make sure that their practice meets all regulations of their state(s). Telehealth and, most recently, the utilization of AI can present liability issues. Nurse attorneys are the perfect solution to help ensure that the NP chooses the correct entity and understands all the regulations that need to be met, including but not limited to zoning requirements, marketing, advertising, and social media.

***

ALTERNATIVE DISPUTE RESOLUTION

Paula DiMeo Grant, RN, BSN, MA, JD

DISCLOSURE

THE AUTHOR HAS NO FINANCIAL INTERESTS OR RELATIONSHIPS WITH ANY OF THE PRODUCTS OR PROGRAMS SUGGESTED IN THIS CHAPTER, NOR DO THEY ENDORSE THEM.

DISCLAIMER

WHILE THIS CHAPTER GUIDEBOOK OFFERS GUIDANCE ON SOLO PRACTICE, IT SHOULD NOT BE CONSTRUED AS LEGAL ADVICE.

There are three time-tested alternative dispute resolution (ADR) methods that can be used to resolve disputes. You know them: negotiation, mediation, and arbitration. Mediation and arbitration require the input of a third party, a mediator or arbitrator. The courts often mandate mediation as it is a more efficient and cost-effective way to settle disputes. It is common to see binding arbitration clauses in many contracts. These processes provide disputants with opportunities to resolve conflicts in a manner that is less time-consuming and less expensive than litigation.

NEGOTIATION

By the time you have hung your shingle as a sole practitioner, you are probably very familiar with and adept at negotiating to settle disputes in various settings, both personally and professionally.

Negotiation, unlike mediation and arbitration, does not require the assistance of a third party. It is the least formal ADR method, whereas mediation and arbitration are more formal. When negotiating, keep in mind four basic points.

1. **People:** Separate the people from the problem.
2. **Interests:** Focus on the interests and not positions.
3. **Options:** Generate a variety of possibilities before deciding what to do.
4. **Objectivity:** Insist that the result be based upon some objective standard.

(Source: Fisher & Ury, 1983, p. 11)

NEGOTIATION PRINCIPLES

Nurse Attorney D. M. Boulay has set forth the following negotiation principles. These principles are helpful when preparing to negotiate. Honing your negotiation skills will benefit your practice; the more you negotiate, the better you will get at it.

- Be prepared
- Know your needs
- Set goals

- Recognize all issues
- Identify options
- Choose the best solution
- Determine initial position
- Decide the bottom line
- Determine fallback position
- Know what the other person wants
- Work for a win/win solution
- Watch your words
- Bargain in good faith
- Stay alert and
- Get it in writing

MEDIATION

Mediation is a facilitated negotiation with the assistance of a third party, the mediator. It is the next tool in line after negotiations fail to settle the dispute. The concept of mediation is one of voluntariness and empowering the parties to fashion their own remedies for settlement. The advantages of mediation include its cost-effectiveness, confidentiality, time-saving, and control over the outcome, as well as its ability to sustain or enhance personal relationships. The venue for mediation should be a neutral site. The time frame for mediation depends upon the complexity of the dispute. In court-mandated mediation, the time frame is usually two hours.

TYPES OF MEDIATION

There are three basic types of approaches to mediation:

1. Facilitative: a traditional mediator method to facilitate the parties.
2. Evaluative: an assessment of the strengths and weaknesses of the case.

3. Transformative: An approach that seeks to empower the parties to settle disputes.

The approach used depends upon the parties, the nature of the dispute, and the mediator's skills. The mediator may use more than one approach during mediation, as it may be more advantageous.

PREMEDIATION

Preparation for mediation is the key to a successful outcome. In some cases, the parties agree to mediate the dispute, while in others, the court mandates mediation.

In some instances, as an attorney representing a party to court-mandated mediation, you may be asked to complete a Confidential Settlement Statement (CSS) or the like to be filed with the court and sent to the mediator for mediation purposes only. The CSS allows the mediator the opportunity to get a case perspective from each side. It sets the parameters for settlement. (See Appendix: CSS Form (2017). Source: Superior Court District of Columbia Multi-Door Dispute Resolution Division.)

SIX STAGES OF MEDIATION

1. **Mediator's Opening Statement.** Introductions are made, and the mediator explains the process. The ground rules are discussed, and a time frame is outlined.
2. **Case presentation by the parties or attorneys.** The parties get to give their explanation of the dispute. This stage is also known as information gathering and occurs in a group or joint session.
3. **Issue development and discussion.** The mediator facilitates a discussion of issues raised and assists the parties in reframing them, if necessary, for a better understanding.
4. **Brainstorming/generating options.** The mediator encourages the parties to put forth all options for resolution. This process can take

place in individual or group sessions. The mediator remains cognizant of confidentiality in individual sessions unless permitted to disclose to the other party.

5. **Evaluation of options.** The options identified in the previous stage are discussed and analyzed. We call these alternatives BATNA (best alternative to a negotiated agreement), or WATNA (worst alternative to a negotiated agreement). Source: (Fisher, Ury & Patton, 1991). It has been my experience that the parties end up with something in between.
6. **Agreement is reached.** The goal of mediation is to reach an agreement that is mutually satisfying to the parties and entered into without coercion. When the parties reach an agreement, the terms and conditions are put in writing and signed by the parties. The agreement is a contract and may be enforceable in a court of law if a breach occurs.

Note: This format provides a blueprint for mediation. If the parties do not reach an agreement, the parties may be closer to settlement following mediation. Complex cases may require more than one mediation session. One can conduct mediation by teleconference or other technical means. This is called E-mediation.

ARBITRATION

Unlike mediation, arbitration does not allow the parties to control the outcome of their case.

The parties agree to have an arbitrator, chosen upon agreement, decide to settle their dispute. The arbitration process is similar to a court trial in that counsel usually represents each side, and a third party, an arbitrator, makes a decision. Arbitrators have varied expertise and are bound by procedural rules and confidentiality. They have the authority to decide as a judge or jury would in a court of law. Unlike litigation, arbitration is a private process usually conducted without a court reporter. There are no formal rules regarding evidence; rather, the arbitrator can consider the evidence and weigh admissibility accordingly. There may be pre-arbitration hearing conferences. Arbitration is less costly and less time-consuming than litigation. Arbitration gives an opportunity for early resolution of a dispute. In some instances, there may be a non-binding arbitration that assists the parties in narrowing or clarifying the issues for settlement.

It is common to find arbitration clauses in many contracts, including union employment contracts, with binding arbitration as the last step in the grievance process. In binding arbitration, there may be a right to appeal only in rare circumstances. Appeals may not be made based on merits unless the arbitrator has exceeded authority or there has been fraud or misconduct or any other statutory basis. The parties may agree to conduct some or all of the arbitration hearing by teleconference or other technical means.

Sometimes, practitioners use a combination of mediation and arbitration called Med-Arb to settle disputes. The parties agree to mediate first, and if mediation is unsuccessful, they proceed to binding arbitration.

In conclusion, negotiation, mediation, and arbitration offer disputants an alternative to expensive and time-consuming litigation to settle disputes. ADR has been successful in many areas of the law, including malpractice matters, employment law, family law, bioethics, elder law, disciplinary defense, and workers' compensation. At some point, you may want to expand your practice by becoming a trained mediator or arbitrator. It can be a rewarding experience.

REFERENCES AND RESOURCES

Grant, P. D. (2018). Dispute resolution for nurses. In P. D. Grant & D. C. Ballard, *Law for nurse leaders,* (pp. 303–329). New York, NY: Springer Publishing.

***

REPRESENTING CLIENTS IN CRIMINAL MATTERS

Flynn P. Carey, JD; Adam D. Brown, JD, BSN, RN;
Robert Esgro, JD, R.Ph.

DISCLOSURE

THE AUTHORS HAVE NO FINANCIAL INTERESTS OR RELATIONSHIPS WITH ANY OF THE PRODUCTS OR PROGRAMS SUGGESTED IN THIS CHAPTER, NOR DO THEY ENDORSE THEM.

DISCLAIMER

WHILE THIS CHAPTER GUIDEBOOK OFFERS GUIDANCE ON SOLO PRACTICE, IT SHOULD NOT BE CONSTRUED AS LEGAL ADVICE.

Criminal law is not for the faint of heart and is not an area you should undertake casually. It can be a vastly rewarding experience and deeply impactful to you personally. The first step in practicing criminal defense is becoming an expert in legal ethics. You are duty-bound to protect your client's confidence, unless the law requires or allows you to disclose information. In the course of your representation, you may be privy to information about criminal behavior and other forms of misconduct. If that feels "icky," this may not be the practice area for you.

Some view protecting these confidences and defending even "the worst" of human activity as the pinnacle of defending the Constitution and the principles that form the fabric of democracy. However, you create your own personal ethos, there is a structure and framework to how a criminal case proceeds. The rest is largely strategy in wielding the tools found in case law to defend your client.

"HOW DO YOU REPRESENT THOSE PEOPLE?"

This is an honest question. First and foremost, "those" people are your friends, neighbors, and siblings. No matter where they come from, if they are charged with a non-military crime anywhere in the United States, they receive the protections of the United States Constitution, as well as the Constitution of the State/Territory where the crime was allegedly committed. Say you have a client who openly admits to you that they committed a crime. As a criminal defense attorney, it remains your duty to defend that person to the best of your ability and hold the government to its burden to prove your client's guilt beyond a reasonable doubt.

Failure to zealously advocate for your client, resulting in a conviction, may result in a claim of Ineffective Assistance of Counsel, which is the easiest way to have the case overturned. If you get into a case and discover facets of it that are "repugnant" to you, though rare, you may be able to withdraw. See ABA Model R. 1.6. As we have all encountered, humans are messy, and no matter how messy, they deserve as much dignity as you can afford them, and they are constitutionally entitled to a robust defense.

A NOTE ON FEES

The vast majority of private criminal practitioners use a flat rate fee structure. Many new attorneys dive into this because, in some cases, you can receive non-refundable capital quickly. Know your jurisdiction, though, because in some cases, even basic misdemeanors can last for years. One author practiced all around Georgia, and the Fulton County docket for traffic misdemeanors would routinely see DUI/DWI cases that were more than five (5) years old. On the other hand, some courts have adopted a "rocket docket" to move cases forward very quickly – leaving little room for continuances and delays.

Structure your fees accordingly and consider whether a case is more appropriately billed as a flat fee or an hourly rate case. Some jurisdictions allow the appointment of private counsel, which often involves typical billable hour timekeeping. Almost all jurisdictions prohibit contingency billing for criminal cases, in which a client only pays if an attorney is successful in trial.

PUBLIC DEFENDERS

Public defenders are the backbone of the criminal justice system. They often get a bad rap and are treated poorly, even by other attorneys. Public defenders often get paid far less than nurses, pursuing their practice of law with the same kind of passion that led many to nursing. If criminal defense is your calling, consider becoming a public defender for a couple of years to gain hands-on experience. Alternatively, befriend as many public defenders as you can to learn from their expertise. Even if you do not practice as a public defender before taking on criminal matters, public defenders are a wealth of knowledge, are "repeat players" before specific courts and court divisions and frequently have special insight into how best to represent your client before a given judge. Their volume of cases also allows them to see prosecuting, plea, and sentencing trends over time.

JURISDICTIONAL CONSIDERATIONS

Criminal matters typically involve courts that can issue punishment that limits a person's liberty. On the state level, these courts include municipal courts, county courts, and a host of other court names like "State Court," "Superior Court," "Sessions Court," and the relevant appellate courts. Federal crimes are dealt with in federal courts, including Magistrate and District Courts. Practitioners should be aware of "separate sovereigns." While a defendant cannot typically be tried twice for the same offense, it is possible, in some instances, for both State authorities and Federal authorities to pursue cases arising out of the same factual circumstances.

ORDINANCE VS. MISDEMEANOR VS. FELONY, PENALTIES

Crimes can be classified as ordinances, misdemeanors, felonies, and several other less familiar names, including "high and aggravated misdemeanors," Class A, B, C, etc., "petty" and "grand." It is crucial to understand how a specific jurisdiction classifies offenses, and a practitioner should familiarize himself or herself with sentencing processes. Having command over the types of offenses is critical in several settings. Because different jurisdictions use slightly different definitions, it is important to understand how a specific jurisdiction uses standard terms like misdemeanor and felony. In general, misdemeanors typically are punishable by up to 12 months in jail, and felonies typically are punishable by 1 year or more in prison. (Some jurisdictions, like Arizona, for instance, cap misdemeanors at six months in jail.)

Jails are typically operated locally (city/county), and prisons are operated on a higher scale (state or federal). Although 12 months equates to one year, misdemeanor courts typically sentence in "months," while felonies are sentenced in "years," except in federal court. Federal courts sentence all crimes in months.

There are special cautions when addressing juvenile offenses. Depending on the jurisdiction, child offenders do not commit "crimes," but instead commit "delinquent acts." In some jurisdictions, a minor who pleads "delinquent" to a delinquent act may not have a disclosure obligation when asked on a job application about pleading "guilty" or being "convicted." It is also essential to examine whether acts committed as a minor can be expunged or destroyed.

STAGES OF A CRIMINAL PROSECUTION

This section will discuss the stages within the court system. The outline below is one of general application—the terms vary based on jurisdiction. However, the normal process for adjudicating a case progresses from law enforcement to prosecution review to the court process.

STAGE 1: LAW ENFORCEMENT INVESTIGATION

This can be through a basic investigation by a patrol officer, leading to an arrest or citation, or can be a months or years-long investigation by detectives or agents. Your ability to participate in the investigation varies based on the type of case and whether your client is aware he or she is under investigation. For more complex cases (and often at the federal level), law enforcement and prosecutors work in tandem when preparing a case for arrest or charges.

STATE 2: ARREST WITHOUT A WARRANT/CITATION

Even though an arrest feels "formal" in the sense that the person is likely in handcuffs and jail, these charges are typically brought by a law enforcement officer (not a lawyer). It is sometimes helpful for a new lawyer in this realm to consider an arrest's informal charges.'

STAGE 3: INDICTMENT/ACCUSATION/FILING OF AN "INFORMATION"

Once a prosecuting attorney has had an opportunity to review the case (which could occur in a matter of hours, days, months, or years), the prosecuting office will file one of the documents named earlier. The charges may be the same as what the person was arrested for, or wholly different. These are the "formal charges."

STAGE 4: ARRAIGNMENT

This is your client's formal response to the formal charges. Typically, you will want to plead Not Guilty in order to initiate the discovery process, and in some jurisdictions, the court will not allow your client to plead guilty at an Arraignment. State processes will vary, so this may not be sound advice in your jurisdiction. Just know that an arraignment is the initial formal response to the prosecutor's formal charges.

STAGE 5: DISCOVERY

Criminal discovery is very different from civil discovery and is often very unstructured. Common civil tools like interrogatories and requests for admission are not generally available, and there is typically not an opportunity for the defense to seek "summary judgment."

Some jurisdictions, like Arizona, have "open" discovery, in which a prosecutor is obligated to turn over anything it will use in a prosecution, all witness statements and any exculpatory information. The defense can also request additional information that it cannot reasonably obtain from other sources.

Other jurisdictions have so-called "trial by ambush," in which there is not a general right to extensive discovery. In those states, there is no general right to pre-trial discovery, a practice that can make defending a criminal case very complicated and unpredictable.

STAGE 6: MOTION HEARING

Throughout the case, you may encounter issues that require a motion hearing. Courts vary; in some jurisdictions, the court will set hearings upon request. In others, there are "law and motion days" in which substantive arguments are heard. Yet, in others, motions "abide trial" and the trial judge will hear all case-related motions at the time of setting the trial. The timing is obviously important—deciding when to deploy an argument or motion is a critical strategy decision.

STAGE 7: PLEA BARGAINING

The reality is that most cases resolve with a plea, and a mere fraction of cases go to trial. Throughout the case, even in cases that are going to trial, a defense practitioner should be thinking about and talking with his or her client about possible plea agreements. A "good" plea should make the client struggle with whether to accept it. Often, pleas allow for certainty of an outcome and remove the unpredictability that can arise when a jury or judge is allowed to decide a sentence. Regardless of the plea extended, a criminal defense attorney must convey any plea offers and obtain appropriate informed consent from the client about accepting or rejecting a plea.

STAGE 8: TRIAL

A trial is the opportunity for the government to attempt to prove its case, and for the defense to either offer an alternative theory that exonerates or excuses the defendant or to undermine or challenge the evidence presented by the government. Recall, the burden remains on the government to prove any offense (and at times, all elements of the offense) beyond a reasonable doubt. The criminal defense attorneys should be careful to prevent any attempt to shift the burden of proof onto the defense. While the goal is to win at trial, criminal defense attorneys also must be ever vigilant to make a clear record and object whenever appropriate. Protection of the record is critical in the post-conviction and appeal stages.

STAGE 9: SENTENCING

If the client takes a plea or is found guilty, they will proceed to sentencing. At this stage, mitigation and rehabilitation are important—criminal defense counsel should think about and develop mitigation and rehabilitation throughout the case. Waiting until a trial loss or entry of a plea is often too late to develop meaningful mitigation.

STAGE 10: APPEAL AND POST-CONVICTION PROCEDURES

There are functionally two components of "post-conviction" proceedings: appeals, which attack legal issues that occurred during trial, and post-conviction relief, which is typically used for broader issues, such as errors in sentencing, ineffective assistance of counsel, and other systemic or major breakdowns in the process. Each has different legal approaches and deadlines.

IMPORTANT NOTE FOR REPRESENTING LICENSEES WHO ARE UNDER THE THREAT OF CRIMINAL PROSECUTION

It is important to separate the cases (criminal defense and licensure defense) in your thought process. A licensing case will have wholly different obligations and strategies from a criminal case. In a criminal case, your client has the right to remain silent, and they should. In a licensing case, your client may well have an obligation to participate in the investigation in order to avoid sanctions from their licensing board. The obligations and consequences in these situations may conflict, and the attorneys representing the client must collaborate in these situations. The criminal case will typically take the driver's seat, but make sure your client understands and makes that decision with you.

There will always be tension between one's liberty interest (in the criminal matter) and one's property interest (in the licensing matter). The general rule is that one cannot be penalized for invoking one's right to remain silent, Spevack v. Klein, 385 U.S. 511, 515, 87 S. Ct. 625, 628 (1967). The Supreme Court expanded this to administrative/civil proceedings. Lefkowitz v. Turley, 414 U.S. 70, 77, 94 S. Ct. 316, 322, 38 L. Ed. 2d 274 (1973). "[A] State may not impose substantial penalties because a witness elects to exercise his Fifth Amendment." Lefkowitz v. Cunningham, 431 U.S. 801, 805, 97 S. Ct. 2132, 2135–36, 53 L. Ed. 2d 1 (1977). A "penalty" is any sanction that makes the assertion of the right costly. Spevack, 385 U.S. at 515, 87 S. Ct. at 628. This includes loss of a professional license. Id.; see also Wohlstrom v. Buchanan, 180 Ariz. 389, 391, 884 P.2d 687, 689 (1994).

An attorney defending a licensee should consider whether to invoke the right to remain silent, since there are a myriad of pros and cons to that strategy. One should also bear in mind that jurisdictions vary on whether someone invokes in a civil or administrative setting, and the finder of fact (such as a board or administrative judge) can draw a "negative inference" about that decision to invoke.

IMPACT ON LICENSEES

A board's general charge is to protect the public and regulate the practice of the given profession. This is a law enforcement function, but boards are NOT general law enforcement agencies. Typically, the scope of a board's authority is limited to the regulation of issues that could or do impact one's ability to practice or the safety of a licensee's patients.

Consideration of crimes that occur in conjunction with the practice of the profession is almost certainly within a board's scope to investigate. Arguably, crimes involving DUI, substance abuse, or the possession of illegal substances, in which a professional's judgment may be impaired, will warrant board consideration.

Some offenses, however, may lack a "nexus" with the practice of the profession. Attorneys should be prepared to not only defend a licensee on the substantive issues but also be mindful of whether a board is within its scope in investigating and taking action against a licensee for criminal conduct unrelated to the practice of the profession.

In addition, some jurisdictions have a statutory "bar" where a licensee is removed from practice upon conviction of certain offenses. This statutory bar may be delegated to a separate entity and may not be under the purview of the licensing board. Before accepting any plea or going to trial, a licensee must be informed about possible collateral consequences.

Certain criminal offenses—including crimes involving substance abuse, abuse of patients, commission of fraud in relation to the delivery of healthcare services, etc. —can result in a mandatory or discretionary exclusion by the United States Department of Health Services. When that occurs, a licensee may be able to maintain their license but will be excluded from participating in federal (and at times, state) healthcare insurance plans. This can be fatal to one's ability to practice.

In addition, for those individuals with prescribing authority from the DEA, felonies and crimes involving controlled substances can result in the DEA seeking to revoke a licensee's prescribing authority.

DUTY TO DISCLOSE TO THE BOARD

Be aware of what triggers the duty to disclose; is it the arrest, the disposition, or the plea? In some states, an arrest triggers the duty to disclose. In others, for example, in Arizona, the duty to report is triggered upon charges being filed. In contrast, in other states, like Michigan and Ohio, entering any plea other than "not guilty" triggers the notification requirement. Some states require reporting at the time of conviction. Still, some other states require disclosure upon renewal of the professional license.

Many criminal defense attorneys erroneously advise their clients that they do not need to tell anyone about a pending criminal case. It is critical to know your licensing authorities and disclose only what is necessary when it is appropriate.

Licensing boards can access, and in some cases are notified by the arresting agencies, information that a licensee has been arrested and/or charged with violation of a criminal statute(s). As such, it is important that the criminal attorney appreciate the notification requirements to avoid an additional allegation that the licensee failed to notify/report to the licensing board in a timely manner.

EXPUNGEMENT OF CRIMINAL RECORDS

If expungement of a criminal record is available, it's an excellent idea. However, it may have limited benefits to a licensee. Some jurisdictions require the guilty party to wait up to five years until they can apply for an expungement, long after a board notification is required. Also, regardless of an expungement, many licensing boards will require a licensee to self-report the events of an arrest, plea or conviction.

Many licensing boards require fingerprinting at the time of initial licensure. In those jurisdictions, the licensing board will capture police fingerprinting at the time of an arrest.

In the criminal realm, there are an immeasurable number of ways to close a case. From bottom to top, in rough order of preference, here are the desired outcomes for licensees, with several options in each category:

1. No arrest
2. Outright dismissal
3. Dismissal following "informal" pre-trial diversion program (not on the record)
4. Dismissal based on suppression of illegally obtained evidence (some states will not allow these charges to be expunged/restricted, but it's still a win for licensing purposes).
5. Not guilty on all charges
6. Not guilty on the impactful charges
7. Reducing charges as much as possible—some will have no impact, and some will have some impact.
8. "Programs" to avoid state-level felony conviction, but will still have consequences (first offender, conditional discharge, "formal" post-plea pre-trial diversion, etc.). These programs are not honored by federal law and will likely be considered a disposition for a felony.

A NOTE ON "TREATMENT"

Suppose you have a client who faces criminal charges and who also provides healthcare services to others, and your client needs treatment. In that case, it may be favorable in both settings to proactively guide a client to treatment services. However, many licensing boards require disclosure of these diversion treatment programs and may initiate discipline immediately upon notification of the diversion program.

In addition, if a licensing board orders a licensee to be tested, screened, or evaluated, the licensee may be compelled to disclose any new pending criminal charges, the fact of, and possibly the details of, one's treatment.

When treatment is considered, it is important to get informed consent from the licensee-client, including informing the client how their statements in treatment may be used.

CONCLUSION

In closing, criminal defense is a challenging and rewarding area of practice. You should not undertake it lightly. Sometimes, people misconstrue that criminal defense is easier to navigate due to the lack of structure compared to civil litigation. However, when done correctly, it serves an important societal interest and can protect clients and licensees facing potential loss of freedom or licensure.

***

DISCIPLINARY DEFENSE

Teressa M. Sanzio, RN, MPA, JD; Paula DiMeo Grant, RN, BSN, MA, JD; Melanie L. Balestra, NP, JD; Karen J. Halpern, RN, BSN, MSN, JD

DISCLOSURE

THE AUTHORS HAVE NO FINANCIAL INTERESTS OR RELATIONSHIPS WITH ANY OF THE PRODUCTS OR PROGRAMS SUGGESTED IN THIS CHAPTER, NOR DO THEY ENDORSE THEM.

DISCLAIMER

WHILE THIS CHAPTER GUIDEBOOK OFFERS GUIDANCE ON SOLO PRACTICE, IT SHOULD NOT BE CONSTRUED AS LEGAL ADVICE.

OVERALL SECTION NOTE: *While the focus of this section is on the representation of nurses, the information contained herein would also apply to other health care professionals.*

When forming a licensure defense practice, first, familiarize yourself with your state Nurse Practice Act. Next, research the investigation/disciplinary procedure in your State. If possible, try to find an experienced nurse attorney who will mentor you through the process. Also, stay connected to the TAANA list serve. That can be a valuable source of helpful information.

LICENSURE DEFENSE CLIENT DEVELOPMENT

Having a professional website is an excellent way to build a practice. The website should comply with your state's attorney advertising rules. Consider hiring a skilled webmaster to assist you in setting up the website rather than the "do-it-yourself" type of website. The website is your representation to the public. You want to project professionalism. [For additional information on Marketing, refer to Chapter 3.]

Many forms of advertising will attract clients for licensure defense cases. Some include presenting lectures at Schools of Nursing and professional nursing organizations; introducing yourself to Substance Use Disorder Programs/Alternative to Discipline groups and insurance panels; and publishing in professional journals on topics related to licensure defense and/or professional discipline.

SCREEN CASE & INATAKE MEETING

Screen all cases to make sure you are competent to handle them. First, perform a conflict check. Second, you should research every potential client by checking their licensure status in all jurisdictions where they were licensed for prior discipline. Check the Medicaid/Medicare exclusion lists and research the NURSYS data bank. While you will ask the client about these issues during the intake meeting, it is best to "trust but verify." Don't make promises you cannot keep. (See Chapter 4, Scope of Practice, for additional information).

REPRESENTATION BY COUNSEL

Upon completion of a conflicts check and if you decide to represent the client, execute a Representation Agreement. This is discussed in greater detail in Chapter 5. Generally, however, the Representation Agreement should be specific as to the terms and conditions of the representation, including fees, and the scope of representation.

A client should never have direct contact with anyone from the disciplinary agency once counsel represents them. You should clearly stipulate this in the representation agreement. Instruct your client that once they retain you, they should have no further direct communication with the agency. Also, instruct your client to refrain from discussing the case with anyone unless otherwise instructed by counsel.

Ask your client to create a personal file, including any/all documentation concerning the issue that forms the basis for the discipline. Include all CEUs, awards, letters of reference, performance evaluations, witness information [statements, contact information]. The client should continue to add to this file during the pendency of the matter. There may be instances when the client may need to obtain a copy of their personnel file.

THE DISCIPLINARY AGENCY INTERVIEW

If your state permits an in-person interview with the disciplinary investigator, make sure to thoroughly prepare the client for the interview and accompany the client to the interview. If your state permits a file review prior to the interview, make sure to schedule a file review with the agency in advance of the interview so you know the information the agency has already obtained. You should have a prep meeting with your client prior to the interview and not on the same day. Schedule the prep meeting a few days to a week before the interview, allowing the client time to recall any forgotten information or to clarify any outstanding issues. We cannot stress the value of thorough preparation enough. If you conduct the prep conference too far in advance, the client may forget the key points. Also, advise your client that their physical presentation, attire, and demeanor are being assessed at an in-person interview. The client should be professionally attired and speak clearly and directly while maintaining appropriate eye contact and composure.

If you have a choice on whether or not the interview will be recorded, consider whether you would permit the client to give a recorded statement. There are two schools of thought on this issue. Some attorneys do not permit recordings because the client may make an admission that is not expected or is problematic, and which is memorialized and can potentially impede the defense. Also, the client is now locked in testimony before discovery can be completed. Other lawyers permit recordings with the thought that memorialization early on eliminates confusion and misinterpretation. This is a personal choice made by the attorney.

NEGOTIATION AND RESOLUTION OF THE CASE

Thoughtful negotiation can resolve many cases. If a settlement is not possible, then the client has the right to a hearing or other administrative process. Be sure to review the Administrative Procedures Act [APA] for procedures and time deadlines. Consider all options thoughtfully and discuss these fully with the client. (See ADR Section of this chapter.)

SPECIAL CONSIDERATIONS

Consideration for Cases with a Criminal Component

Often, disciplinary defense involves representation of a licensee who has been charged with a crime. In several jurisdictions, a licensee is required to report an arrest and/or conviction to the licensing agency within a statutory timeframe. Failure to report could be considered a violation of the law. Some jurisdictions bar the practice of nursing when convicted of a felony. We highly recommend that when representing a nurse with an arrest/conviction, you work closely with an experienced criminal defense attorney when structuring a plea agreement. Certain convictions may impact the licensee's ability to practice.

Consideration for Impaired Providers

If your client has a substance use disorder and/or a mental or physical condition that may impact their ability to practice, it may require agency monitoring. Determine if your State offers an alternative to a discipline program. These programs are designed to strictly monitor the nurse to ensure safety and competency to practice over a designated time. If the nurse successfully completes the program, they will not have a disciplinary action on their license. The alternative to a discipline program is typically confidential, and the nurse is not reported to the mandated reporting agencies. If a nurse violates any term of the program, the consequences could be serious, including the lifting of confidentiality and subsequent reporting of disciplinary action, which may include revocation of a license.

When screening potential clients, be sure to gather information related to criminal background and medical/mental health history, including prescribed medications. Matters involving DUIs or allegations of diversion or impairment on duty will typically require the licensee to undergo a fitness for duty evaluation (psychological/neuropsychological). Knowing your clients' medical/mental health history (including chemical dependency) will be useful in preparing your client and defending the case.

Considerations for Advanced Practice Nurses

Advanced practice nurses are subject to Board complaints and investigations, as well. When representing advanced practice nurses, determine if the jurisdiction allows for independent or collaborative practice. Any settled malpractice case will automatically be reported to the Board of Nursing, which will likely trigger an investigation, and which may result in disciplinary action taken by the Board.

Consideration of the Enhanced Nurse Licensure Compact and Pending Advanced Practice Registered Nurse Compact

There are currently 34 States that participate in the Enhanced Nurse Licensure Compact (see Appendix for list of participating States). Determine if the State where you practice and represent nurses is part of the compact. Become familiar with the verbiage, the definitions of home state, remote state, and adverse actions that can be taken against both the license and the privilege. To avoid or mitigate disciplinary action on either the license or the privilege, you must be knowledgeable of the statutes and rules in both the home state and the remote state that grants the privilege to practice. The National Council of State Boards of Nursing (NCSBN) adopted the Advanced Practice Registered Nurse Compact on August 12, 2020. It will become effective when seven party States enact it. NCSBN offers a wealth of information on the Nurse Compacts.

CONSEQUENCES OF LICENSURE DISCIPLINE

Be aware that each State where a nurse holds a license may be the subject of disciplinary action in that State, which is derivative of an action taken in any State. This is the case even if a license is lapsed or expired. In addition to reciprocal enforcement (derivative action), disciplinary actions are reported to the National Practitioner Data Bank, NURSYS, and, depending on the nature of the case, can be reported to the Office of the Inspector General, the Drug Enforcement Agency, Medicare, and State Medicaid.

Disciplinary action against a licensee can negatively impact employability and the ability to obtain insurance. For the Nurse Practitioner, disciplinary action may impact privileging and approval on insurance panels. This can also impact practice areas such as telemedicine and traveling nurse work.

In some cases, prior disciplinary action is also used against the nurse for future conduct. The financial impact goes without saying, and the emotional turmoil is profound. It is demoralizing, humiliating, and it is in the public domain.

NSO/HPSO BILLING

TAANA and NSO/HPSO maintain a strategic alliance. TAANA's association with NSO/HPSO encourages members to be on a referral list. NSO/HPSO reimburses TAANA attorneys $200.00/hour for representation, except for representing massage therapists; reimbursement is $150.00/hour. Other insurance companies may reimburse the attorney a different amount. Either higher or lower. Ultimately, the attorney decides the hourly rate to charge a client, notwithstanding insurance reimbursement rates.

RESOURCES FOR REPRESENTING NURSES IN DISCIPLINARY MATTERS

The following resources may be helpful in representing nurses in disciplinary matters:

- Nurse Practice Act
- Administrative Procedures Act
- eNLC
- ANA Standards of Practice

- ANA Code of Ethics
- Agency Rules and Regulations
- Employment Manuals
- Previous BON decisions

ENHANCED NURSING LICENSURE COMPACT

In 1999, the National Licensure Compact (NLC) was formed and approved by the National Council of State Boards of Nursing (NCSBN) to facilitate the practice of Registered Nurses (RNs) and Licensed Practical/Vocational Nurses (LPNs/VNs) across state lines through a streamlined licensure process without additional paperwork or added fees for multiple licenses. To be eligible for a Compact or multistate license, the nurse must declare a Compact state as a primary residence and hold an active license to practice nursing in good standing. A primary residence state is also referred to as the "home state." The nurse can only have one primary residence at a time and is obligated to notify the Board of Nursing (BON) should a move occur. In 2015, twenty-five (25) states comprised the original NLC.

In May 2015, the NCSBN adopted the Enhanced Nurse Licensure Compact (eLNC), which revised and improved the original NLC. Among the improvements are uniform licensure requirements as well as state and federal criminal background checks and licensure restrictions on nurses with felony convictions. It also provides for a sharing of disciplinary actions among participating states in a coordinated manner. Thus, the new Compact was implemented on January 19, 2018, and party states were deemed withdrawn from the original or "Prior Compact." Nurses holding a multistate license on July 20, 2017, were grandfathered into the eNLC, allowing them to practice in all member states (NCSBN 2018). To date, 35 member states are participating in this Compact. (NCSBN 2020).

INTERSTATE COMMISSION OF NURSE LICENSURE COMPACT ADMINISTRATORS

An Interstate Commission of Nurse Licensure Compact Administrators (ICNLCA) was formed in 2017 and is the governing body of the NLC. This commission is considered a quasi-governmental and joint public agency of the party states (NCSBN, 2018).

The ICNLCA's purpose and duties are described in Article VII of NLC.

DISCIPLINARY MEASURES

The framework for the disciplinary process may be found in Article V of the NLC, titled "Additional Authorities Invested in Party State Licensing Board," and Article VI, titled "Coordinated Licensure Information System and Exchange of Information." In addressing disciplinary actions by state Boards of Nursing (BON), Article V gives broad authority to both home and party states regarding adverse disciplinary actions taken against nurses. The goal here is to ensure public safety.

Article V of the Compact states in part:

...a licensing board shall have authority to:

1. Take adverse action against a nurse's multistate licensure privilege to practice within the party state.
   i. Only the home state shall have the power to take adverse action against a nurse's license issued by the home state.
   ii. For purposes of taking adverse action, the home state licensing board shall give the same priority and effect to reported conduct received from a remote state as it would if such conduct had occurred within the home state. In doing so, the home state shall apply its own state laws to determine the appropriate action (NCSBN, NLC 2015, pp. 6, 7).

iii. Article V, 7 (b), further states, "[I]f adverse action is taken by the home state against a nurse's multistate license, the nurse's multistate licensure privileges to practice in all party states shall be deactivated until all encumbrances have been removed from the multistate license..." (NCSBN, NLC 2015, p 7).

Article VI of the Compact requires that all party states participate in a coordinated licensure information system regarding the licensure and disciplinary actions of all nurses. In some instances, state law may deem this information confidential.

ADVANCED PRACTICE REGISTERED NURSES COMPACT (APRN)

In 2015, the NCSBN developed and approved model legislation to be enacted by the states, enabling APRNs to practice across state lines in other Compact states with one multistate license similar to the privileges afforded to RNs and LPN/VNs by the NLC. The NCSBN Delegate Assembly adopted the APRN Compact on August 20, 2020.

The APRN Compact consists of eleven (11) Articles. Its general purpose is to facilitate the states' responsibility to protect the public's health and safety, ensure the cooperation of party states in areas of APRN licensure, and regulate and promote uniform licensure requirements.

The APRN Compact will become effective when it is enacted into law by seven (7) states (APRN Compact, 2020). It is a work in progress.

For additional information on NLC and APRN Compact, see:

ncsbn.org

ncsbn.org/nurse-licensure compact.htm

ncsbn.org/aprn-compact.htm

REFERENCES AND RESOURCES

- APRN Licensure Compact (August 12, 2020). Retrieved from https://www.ncsbn.org/nurse-licensure compact.htm
- News Release: NCSBN Enhanced Nurse Licensure Compact (eNLC) Implemented Jan. 19, 2018. Retrieved from https://NCSBN.org
- Nurse Licensure Compact (May 4, 2015). Retrieved from https://www.ncsbn.org/nurse licensure-compact.htm
- Oyleye, O.A., (May 20, 2019) "The Nursing Licensure Compact and Its Disciplinary Provisions: What Nurses Should Know" *OJIN: The Online Journal of Issues in Nursing Vol. 24, No. 2.*

***

EMPLOYMENT LAW

Kathleen A. McCormac, BSN, JD

DISCLOSURE

THE AUTHOR HAS NO FINANCIAL INTERESTS OR RELATIONSHIPS WITH ANY OF THE PRODUCTS OR PROGRAMS SUGGESTED IN THIS CHAPTER, NOR DO THEY ENDORSE THEM.

DISCLAIMER

WHILE THIS CHAPTER GUIDEBOOK OFFERS GUIDANCE ON SOLO PRACTICE, IT SHOULD NOT BE CONSTRUED AS LEGAL ADVICE.

Working with clients in employment law matters is interesting and challenging work for solo practitioners. Most claims involve underlying issues of discrimination, harassment, or retaliation at work. Breach of contract, fair pay, family medical leave, and wage and hour claims may also require the engagement of employment lawyers.

OVERVIEW OF DISCRIMINATION CLAIMS

Title VII of the Civil Rights Act of 1964, 42 USC §§2000e-2000e17, provides the basis of protection for workers from discrimination in employment. Most states have parallel or more expansive protection under the State Codes. It is important to determine what venue is best or appropriate for filing your client's case, Federal or State Court.

FILING PROCEDURE

You must file all claims with the Equal Employment Opportunity Commission (EEOC). The employee will be interviewed, or the attorney can prepare an affidavit in response to the charge. The Employer's attorney must file a response to the EEOC charge once the EEOC serves it. There are strict statutory guidelines that affect the timing of filing with the EEOC. They provide that an employee may need to file within 180 or 300 days, depending on the allegations. State statutes may provide a longer time to file. Employees must be advised of these limitations even if the attorney decides not to represent them.

Many states allow additional time to file charges and will cross-file with the EEOC. It is important to determine when the discriminatory conduct occurred, whether it is ongoing, and when the last incident of discrimination occurred. The EEOC may investigate the claim and issue a finding. They may also attempt to have the parties resolve the dispute through conciliation or mediation at no charge to the parties. The EEOC may, instead of or after failure of the voluntary resolution process, issue a Right to Sue. The employee will have as few as 90 days under the Federal Statute 42 USC §2000e-5(f)(1) to file a civil complaint after receiving the Right to Sue. State statutes may provide a longer time to file.

TYPES OF CLAIMS

Individuals are protected from discrimination based on disability, age, gender, race, national origin, sexual orientation (in some States), whistleblowing, sexual harassment, and pay inequity in employment. The burden is on the employee to prove the discrimination and damages, but the level of the burden differs depending on the alleged conduct. Disability discrimination claims do not require the Employee to prove discriminatory animus, whereas allegations of race discrimination require proof of animus.

Title VII Claims generally fall into the following categories:

- Individual "disparate treatment"
- Retaliation
- Disparate Impact of Adverse Impact
- Class-wide pattern and practice
- Hostile environment

EXCLUSIONS

Some employers are exempt from the Title VII definition of employer, including the US Federal Government and Indian tribes. Employers must have 15 employees in order for most claims to be made by an employee. Individual employees, such as supervisors, cannot be held liable under Title VII.

There are state statutes that cover smaller employers and other claims that may be made against supervisors.

DAMAGES

Plaintiffs may claim lost income, benefits, general pain and suffering damages, and attorney fees and costs. Under TITLE VII claims, the general damages are limited to $300,000.00; however, states may allow for greater amounts.

LITIGATION

These cases can be factually intensive, which reduces the chance of a summary judgment dismissal. A practitioner must be prepared for discovery and trial or arbitration of any employment claims.

***

ESTATE PLANNING LAW PRACTICE

Conswella M. Byrd RN, BSN, JD

DISCLOSURE

THE AUTHOR HAS NO FINANCIAL INTERESTS OR RELATIONSHIPS WITH ANY OF THE PRODUCTS OR PROGRAMS SUGGESTED IN THIS CHAPTER, NOR DO THEY ENDORSE THEM.

DISCLAIMER

WHILE THIS CHAPTER GUIDEBOOK OFFERS GUIDANCE ON SOLO PRACTICE, IT SHOULD NOT BE CONSTRUED AS LEGAL ADVICE.

WHAT IS ESTATE PLANNING?

An estate comprises the assets a person accumulates during their lifetime: home, car, bank accounts, investments, jewelry, furniture, a business, etc. An estate plan is a plan made in advance of two major life events: death and incapacity.

An estate plan includes written instructions stating who the beneficiaries are that will receive all or some of the estate, what they will receive and when they will receive it. In this way, an estate plan provides for a guardian and inheritance manager for minor children; transfer of a business; coordination of assets distribution; providing for dependents; tax planning; and more.

Good estate planning should also include planning for the second major life event: incapacity. This part of estate planning can be achieved through a variety of legal documents that allow a person to designate another to act for them at a time when they are alive but mentally unable to make decisions for themselves.

Everyone in the US has an estate plan: the one that a person makes for their estate or the one that the state of residency makes for them, which is a probate regarding distribution of assets and a conservatorship regarding decision making at a time of mental incapacity. Estate planning should include all the areas of a person's life that would be affected if they were no longer alive or if they were suffering from mental incapacity. It is a process, not a document, and it needs to change as a person's situation and the laws change.

WHY CHOOSE AN ESTATE PLANNING LAW PRACTICE?

Many will assume that, as a nurse attorney, your law practice will be in the areas of medical and/or nursing malpractice and defense, personal injury, or healthcare law because these areas involve the obvious combination of a nursing background and the law. Estate planning deals with death and dying and mental incapacity, and the law.

If you are thinking about starting your own legal practice or if you have a solo firm and are looking to expand into a new area of law, estate planning is a great place to start. The range of legal services included in an estate planning practice is uniquely suited to small and solo firms, and they can accommodate more flexible work environments. Estate planning can become complex, but most clients require a relatively straightforward and defined set of legal solutions.

HOW TO ESTABLISH AN ESTATE PLANNING LAW PRACTICE

The first step in starting an estate planning practice is to educate yourself about the area of law. Estate planning encompasses state-specific probate and trust laws, as well as state and federal tax laws. You may start educating yourself by buying a few estate planning books or attending your state's continuing legal education seminar. If you have access to a network of attorneys in your area, start attending events for estate planning professionals. Your state's bar association likely has an estate planning group that provides educational and networking events, and some even have an email listserv on which attorneys discuss legal questions.

- There are online tools that people use to draft their own DIY wills, trusts, and durable powers of attorney. These tools may make it seem like estate planning legal services are merely about interviewing clients and filling out forms. In reality, providing quality estate planning services is more complicated than that. As an attorney, you can provide carefully tailored and individualized advice to clients based on their assets, family structure, and future goals. However, that does not mean that you are unable to utilize drafting software or template documents as a starting point. Drafting software such as Matthew Bender, Lexis Nexis, and Trust and Wealth Counsel can be a useful tool to support your legal work. If you prefer working with a human, companies like Back Office Drafter (Laney Lyons-Richardson) offer drafting assistance.
- The second step is to draft a vision for your estate planning law practice. It is important to identify your goals, values, and preferences for your estate planning law practice. Without clearly set goals, it is easy to get distracted, lose focus, and end up moving away from the reasons you started your estate planning law practice.
- The third step is putting all of the pieces in play. Create a legal entity, obtain an EIN, open a trust bank account, hire an accountant, establish a website, decide where you are going to meet clients, where you are going to work, and with whom, purchase malpractice insurance, client management software, estate planning drafting software, office equipment, and supplies. We describe most of

these topics in this guidebook, so I will focus on those related to estate planning law practice issues.

OBTAINING CLIENTS

Since everyone needs estate planning, there are a variety of referral sources available to you. An important category is professionals who manage other people's money, but do not practice law, such as life insurance agents and financial planners. They need an estate planning attorney to whom they can refer their clients for their estate planning needs.

Your existing and former clients will welcome the news that they can hire a familiar attorney to handle their estate planning. You should create or purchase client-oriented information brochures on estate planning from estate planning information companies such as Schumacher Publishing, to send to them. Christmas or Holiday cards can serve as an annual reminder that you care and are still in business.

Other attorneys who do not practice estate planning are good referral sources. They need an estate planning attorney for mutual business referrals.

Nurse attorneys are usually welcomed to provide estate planning seminars to local NP groups and organizations, and write estate planning articles for NP online groups, newsletters, and magazines. Most nurses prefer hiring a nurse attorney to provide their estate planning because their dual background in nursing and law allows nurse attorneys to provide more support and understanding during the estate planning process, especially when discussing sensitive topics like end-of-life wishes.

Creating and maintaining a professional website is an essential resource for potential clients. It will help potential clients who search the web for an estate planning attorney find you. It is best to have a professional web design company specializing in estate planning marketing, create and maintain your website so that it can be updated to include the changes in the laws.

MEETING WITH CLIENTS

Many estate planning attorneys meet with their clients in their law office. Due to the nature of estate planning, you may have to meet with clients in their homes or hospital rooms because they may have difficulty getting to your office. In that case, it is important to determine testamentary capacity and the presence of undue influence.

Identifying exactly who your client is presents some unique issues to estate planning. If you represent both spouses, you must discuss spousal dual legal representation and obtain a waiver of conflict of interest.

If the adult children have contacted you, you must make it clear that the parent, not the adult children, is your client, even if the adult children pay for your legal services. In that case, it is crucial to determine testamentary capacity and the presence of undue influence. If you are concerned, be careful to protect yourself. You may need to have the client evaluated before you accept them as your client.

Your meeting should only be with the client(s), not others, due to the attorney-client privilege. This is also important because clients need to be open with you. To avoid the appearance of or actual undue influence, it is best to have others wait outside the meeting room.

ANALYZE CLIENT INFORMATION AND DEVELOP AN ESTATE PLAN

To analyze the client's assets and develop an estate plan, it is necessary to obtain the client's information regarding the client's family, assets, and liabilities. The client should complete your client intake form before meeting with you. In this way, you can spend the meeting time discussing your client's particular needs, without spending time obtaining information from them. Additionally, the client can spend time outside the meeting obtaining the correct information without wasting meeting time. You cannot begin to assess a client's estate planning needs until you have all of their information and know what they want, require, and need.

Estate planning drafting software usually includes a client intake form, in addition to client letters and supporting documents. I have included the intake form that I use in my estate planning law practice at the end of this section.

Once you have obtained the necessary information and determined your client's objectives, you should analyze their situation and develop an estate plan accordingly. This guidebook does not teach you how to develop an estate plan. Here are five points I have found to be effective in guiding you.

- First, explain your analysis to your client(s). Whatever estate planning you determine that your clients require, you must communicate and explain your analysis to them. If they agree, you can prepare the suggested plan. They may have suggestions and/or modifications. It is important to remember that it is their estate plan, not yours.
- Second, once you and the client agree to the proposed plan of action, you must prepare an engagement letter detailing precisely what you will and will not be doing, what you will be charging for your services, when the payment will be due, and conflict of interest waivers. It is important to resolve disputes before there is a problem. The estate planning drafting software should include sample engagement letters and other documents to guide you. However, you must refer to your State Bar letter of engagement requirements.
- Third, complete an internal checklist of things you will do and use it as a guide to ensure that you have completed what you have

agreed to do. Without an internal checklist, it will be easy to miss the many required details in estate planning.

- Fourth, it is common practice to prepare a first draft of the agreed-upon estate planning documents and the supporting documents and send them to the client for review, approval, and return them to you with any additional requested information. Some clients prefer to review them at home, while others prefer to review them with you in your law office.
- Fifth is the final meeting with the client. Traditionally, the final estate planning documents are printed on paper containing at least 25% cotton so that they will not "yellow" over time and are enclosed with a cover. Many estate planning office supply companies can provide these supplies.
- Most estate planning documents require the client's signature to be notarized. Many estate planning attorneys and/or their staff are also notaries who provide this service to the client and facilitate the signing process. You can contact the National Notary Association for information about becoming a notary in your state.

In California, the testator's signature on a non-holographic will is required to be witnessed by at least two witnesses who are not beneficiaries of the will and/or estate. Available staff or others who can be witnesses to the non-holographic will are an important consideration when deciding the location of your law office.

In California, estate planning attorneys are not required to keep any of the client's final, original executed client documents. Advise your clients to store them in a safe place, such as a safe deposit box.

I have been an estate planning attorney since 1990. I have found it to be a gratifying career that has allowed me to serve my community in ways that are fulfilling for both of us. If you choose a career as an estate planning attorney, I hope you will find the same reward.

REFERENCES AND RESOURCES

1. conswellambyrd.com
2. Wealth Counsel: https://www.wealthcounsel.com/articles/2014/on-making-the-transition-to-estate-planning
3. Estate and Wills Supplies and website hosting: Schumacher Publishing, https://schumacherpublishing.com/
4. Estate and Wills Supplies: Blumberg Legal Automation: https://www.blumberg.com/estate-and-will-planning/EWS
5. Books
    - CEB *Estate Planning for the General Practitioner*
    - CEB, *California Decedent Estate Practice*
    - CEB, *California Trust and Probate Litigation*
    - CEB, *California Trust Administration*
    - Hartog, *California Wills & Trusts* (Lexis/Nexis)
    - Hartog, *California Trust Practice* (Lexis/Nexis)
    - Blaylock, *California Probate Practice* (Lexis/Nexis)
6. Periodicals
    - CEB, *Estate Planning & California Probate Reporter*
    - *California Trust and Estates Quarterly* (State Bar of California, Estate Planning, Trust and Probate Law Section)
    - *Estate Planning Law and Taxation* (WG&L)
7. Articles
    - Evans, "How to Build and Manage and Estate Planning Practice" (Law Practice and Management Section and Section of Real Property, *Probate and Trust Law*, American Bar Association)
    - Leimberg, "Useful Suggestions for Building an Estate Planning Practice." *Estate Planning*, November 1998 (WG&L)

- Soskin, "The Client Interview: A Crucial Tool in Estate Planning." *Estate Planning*, June 2004 (WG&L)
- Blinder & Marshall, When Does Influence Become Undue? CEB, Estate Planning & California Probate Reporter, Vol. 4, No. 2, Summer 1998.

8. Websites
   - LexisNexis: lexisnexis.com—for access to their estate planning books and software, particularly the California Wills & Trust Drafting System, Forms and Text
   - courtinfo.ca.gov—for access to the California Judicial Council forms
   - ceb.com—for access to their estate planning, probate and trust books
9. Software and Law Practice Management
   - Software: LexisNexis: lexisnexis.com—for access to their estate planning books and software, particularly the California Wills & Trust Drafting System, Forms and Text. They also provide state specific software.
   - Software: Wealth Counsel: https://www.wealthcounsel.com/software-for-attorneys
   - Law Practice Management: CLIO: https://www.clio.com/

***

FAMILY LAW

Kim M. Crump, RN, BS, BA, JD

DISCLOSURE

THE AUTHOR HAS NO FINANCIAL INTERESTS OR RELATIONSHIPS WITH ANY OF THE PRODUCTS OR PROGRAMS SUGGESTED IN THIS CHAPTER, NOR DO THEY ENDORSE THEM.

DISCLAIMER
WHILE THIS CHAPTER GUIDEBOOK OFFERS GUIDANCE ON SOLO PRACTICE, IT SHOULD NOT BE CONSTRUED AS LEGAL ADVICE.

SCOPE OF FAMILY PRACTICE & BENEFIT OF NURSING LICENSE

Family law deals with family and the dynamics of family life, including divorce, custody, child abuse and neglect, and adoption. A nursing background can uniquely equip you with skills that would help assist clients, whether you are representing a parent in a divorce or custody battle or representing the interests of a child as the guardian ad litem.

Family law covers a wide range of areas, including divorce, paternity, adoption, and child custody issues, as well as support and domestic violence. Some other unique areas deal with contraception, abortion, intrafamily tort immunity and liability, parental discipline, children in need of supervision, artificial insemination, surrogate motherhood, medical care for a child and spouse, parental liability for the child's acts, and spousal rape.

However, when focusing on the mainstay, there are various ways that having a nursing background can enhance your representation of your clients in family law cases. For example, in divorce and custody matters, nursing skills such as teaching and managing emotions are helpful in resolving disputes and reaching a mutually agreeable solution to address issues. Nurses are equipped with an understanding of psychology, child development, and health promotion, which enables the nurse attorney to find ways to resolve issues using a multidisciplinary approach. In custody cases, understanding the developmental issues of children is crucial.

Most family law attorneys deal not only with the legal issues that clients face but also with the emotional issues that arise from trying to resolve these legal issues. The emotional issues in contested divorce and or custody cases sometimes cloud the litigant's ability to resolve the legal issues. Understanding the client's emotional issues helps resolve the emotional baggage, which in turn facilitates progress in the case. Often, due to emotional issues, clients are unable to move beyond these issues and approach the legal issues rationally. Clients are often not at their best when a contested divorce or custody matter begins, so the lawyer needs to address these emotional upsets when the client is expressing anxiety, depression, or even anger. As a nurse/attorney, you are in a better position to help your client transcend their emotions. You are uniquely qualified to assess the situation, establish ground rules for the relationship, potentially refer clients to other professionals who can help them in coping with these aspects of the litigation process.

In custody cases, the value of having a nursing background becomes evident in evaluating the factors considered when deciding custody cases. Although custody cases are statutorily driven, with uniform child custody laws in most states, the factors that the Court must evaluate require certain objective and subjective decision-making, which is similar to a nursing assessment, such as the factors listed in Virginia Code Section 20-124.3 (1) through (3) (1950) amended. "Best interests" is the keystone in these cases, and the statutory factors that the court has to consider in Virginia weigh in on best interests. The analysis of some of these factors requires making nursing assessments, and the knowledge that nurses have to fully evaluate these factors is helpful.

VIRGINIA CODE SECTION 20-124.3

§ 20-124.3. Best interests of the child; visitation.

In determining best interests of a child for purposes of determining custody or visitation arrangements, including any pendente lite orders pursuant to § 20-103, the court shall consider the following:

1. The age and physical and mental condition of the child, giving due consideration to the child's changing developmental needs;

2. The age and physical and mental condition of each parent;
3. The relationship existing between each parent and each child, giving due consideration to the positive involvement with the child's life, the ability to accurately assess and meet the emotional, intellectual, and physical needs of the child;
4. The needs of the child, giving due consideration to other important relationships of the child, including but not limited to siblings, peers, and extended family members;
5. The role that each parent has played and will play in the future, in the upbringing and care of the child;
6. The propensity of each parent to actively support the child's contact and relationship with the other parent, including whether a parent has unreasonably denied the other parent access to or visitation with the child;
7. The relative willingness and demonstrated ability of each parent to maintain a close and continuing relationship with the child, and the ability of each parent to cooperate in and resolve disputes regarding matters affecting the child;
8. The reasonable preference of the child, if the court deems the child to be of reasonable intelligence, understanding, age, and experience to express such a preference;
9. Any history of (i) family abuse as that term is defined in § 16.1-228; (ii) sexual abuse; (iii) child abuse; or (iv) an act of violence, force, or threat as defined in § 19.2-152.7:1 that occurred no earlier than 10 years prior to the date a petition is filed. If the court finds such a history or act, the court may disregard the factors in subdivision 6; and
10. Such other factors as the court deems necessary and proper to the determination.

The judge shall communicate to the parties the basis of the decision either orally or in writing. Except in cases of consent orders for custody and visitation, this communication shall set forth the judge's findings regarding the relevant factors set forth in this section. At the request of either party, the court may order that the exchange of a child shall take place at an appropriate meeting place.

The goal in custody and visitation cases is to preserve the dignity and resources of the family and to ensure that children have frequent and continuing contact with both of their parents; in other words, the goal is in the best interests of the children.

Counsel should advise the client that all child custody and visitation matters are to be governed by the "best interests" of the child and not those of the parent, and it is important for counsel to help clients establish realistic expectations. If parents cannot reach an agreement concerning their children on their own, they should be advised to consider seeking professional advice from a child development specialist or participating in family counseling to try to reach accommodations that will serve the children's best interests.

Counsel should advise clients that their anger toward the other parent can adversely affect the child and that the client should separate the relationship with the child from the unhappy relationship with the other parent. Indeed, a nurse would be sensitive to and understand these types of issues.

Outside of representing either parent in a custody case, you might be selected to represent the interests of the child as guardian ad litem. Guardian ad litems serve a very valuable purpose in custody cases. They are generally appointed to represent the child's interests in contested custody cases. This is an area where having a nursing background is invaluable, especially when evaluating the factors that the court must look at in determining what is in the best interest of the child. In this role, understanding developmental issues with children is crucial, and nurses are best equipped to do this.

Other areas of family law that nurses are equipped to assist with better are domestic violence, child neglect, and abuse cases. In domestic violence cases, nurses have skills to understand risk factors and the dynamics of family violence, which help in handling cases and finding other options outside of the court system to address and resolve problems. In child neglect and abuse cases, nurses are uniquely qualified to understand anatomy and physiology as well as child development in helping to understand issues of neglect as well as abuse. Such knowledge helps to make determinations regarding issues such as shaken baby syndrome and failure to thrive.

In addition, attorneys working for the Department of Social Services' Child Protective Services handle cases dealing with neglect and abuse. In these cases, having someone with a background in nursing is also invaluable because handling these matters requires an understanding of not only safety concerns for children, but also child development, anatomy and physiology, disorders, and mechanisms of injury. Whether you are representing a parent who has been suspected of causing a child's failure to thrive or whether you are the attorney who is presenting such a case, having the knowledge of these issues is useful.

In addition to helping clients litigate their cases, as a nurse attorney, you can also assist with mediation. Most states, like Virginia, encourage and sometimes require parties to seek a form of mediation to resolve issues, including the attorney mediating, dispute resolution proceedings 8.01-576.4 of the Code of Virginia; separation agreements, and binding arbitration Va. Code 8.01-581.01 to 8.01-581.016 (the Uniform Arbitration Act). There is a newer form of dispute resolution called collaborative law, in which attorneys representing both parties seek to resolve issues without litigation. . As a nurse attorney, you are equipped to sometimes mediate issues with parties in contested divorce/custody cases due to some experience with conflict resolution.

REFERENCES AND RESOURCES

1. Cecka, Dale M., Diehl, Lawrence D. and Cottrell, James Ray, editors. *Virginia Practice Series* (April 2020).
2. Virginia Code Section 20-124.3
3. Lhospital, Dean E., McHugh, Timothy L., editors. *The Virginia Lawyer: A Deskbook For Practitioners*, 6th Edition (2018).
4. Pauline Tesler. *Collaborative Law: Achieving Effective Resolution in Divorce without Litigation.* (2001)

***

HEALTH CARE LAW PRACTICE

Kathleen A. Hessler, RN, Attorney, CHC, CHPC

Contact: khesslerlaw@comcast.net

Randi Kopf, RN, MS, JD

Contact: Kopf@KopfHealthLaw.COM

DISCLOSURE

THE AUTHOR HAS NO FINANCIAL INTERESTS OR RELATIONSHIPS WITH ANY OF THE PRODUCTS OR PROGRAMS SUGGESTED IN THIS CHAPTER, NOR DO THEY ENDORSE THEM.

DISCLAIMER

WHILE THIS CHAPTER GUIDEBOOK OFFERS GUIDANCE ON SOLO PRACTICE, IT SHOULD NOT BE CONSTRUED AS LEGAL ADVICE.

HEALTH CARE LAW DEFINED

A nurse attorney is uniquely qualified to practice health care law. We bring our clinical knowledge and experience to our law practice. We have firsthand experience practicing and working in various health care settings.

Health care law is a field of law that combines administrative and corporate law. A health care law practice can focus on one aspect of this broad area of law, such as fraud and abuse, or you can have a general health law practice that requires a broad knowledge of the laws, regulations, and professional codes. It is often a non-litigation transactional law practice.

There are multiple aspects of health care law, including but not limited to, federal, state and local laws and regulations, case law, advisory opinions, professional codes, rules regarding the practice, delivery and business management of multiple health care professionals and providers, provider entities, the rights of patients, quality of care issues, and the requirements of payment for medical and health care services, including the legal issues regarding relationships between and among providers, practitioners and the payors of healthcare.

HEALTH CARE LAW FOR THE SOLO PRACTITIONER

The scope of health care law is extensive and is one of the most highly regulated, if not the most regulated, areas of law in the United States. As a nurse, you already know some of the applicable laws, such as HIPAA, patient rights, and professional scope of practice. Consequently, it may seem overwhelming for a new solo practitioner to have a general health law practice.

A solo practitioner who wishes to practice health care law may choose to focus on one area of provider representation, such as the acute-care or post-acute care provider, managed care and health care insurance organizations, professional defense, elder law, inpatient or outpatient care, billing fraud and abuse, HIPAA, regulatory compliance/survey management and appeals, or healthcare transactions.

Medical malpractice or wrongful death law (tort law) is not usually included under the umbrella of health care law or regulatory compliance.

However, a lawyer who practices medical malpractice should be aware of the state statutes, professional codes, and regulatory environment that governs hospitals, post-acute care facilities, and health care providers, such as clinics, home health, and hospice agencies. For example, a criminal attorney may get the physician acquitted of charges in a court of law. However, since the charges violated the professional code, the physician still loses their license. In this instance, the health care lawyer's input into the criminal case is an important, if not more important than the criminal lawyer's work, because if the physician loses their license, they can no longer practice medicine.

Negative regulatory findings or survey deficiencies of a provider, such as a physician, hospital, nursing facility, or home care agency, can impact a malpractice or wrongful death case. Also, a lawyer representing hospitals or other healthcare providers may find that they will be consulting with, or sharing regulatory information with, the litigators who represent the same entity or client in malpractice matters.

SOURCES OF HEALTH CARE LAW

Attorneys representing providers or health care entities should also have a general understanding or background in the following areas of law: HIPAA (a lynch pin to health care law practice as it includes compliance with federal and state laws and regulations), professional scope of practice, employment, corporate and transactional law, contract, criminal, and tort law. These areas all potentially intersect with health care law issues. Additionally, health care law practitioners should have a comprehensive understanding of compliance and the government's guidance and expectations regarding provider compliance programs for the practice and reimbursement of covered services. Compliance with HIPAA is no longer limited to privacy, but is interpreted as required compliance with all federal, state, local laws and regulations, as well as electronic security rules.

Further knowledge of advanced directive laws, State Death with Dignity Acts, Living Wills, and Medical Power of Attorney, as well as professional licensing and health care technology, is helpful.

Important sources of health care law include federal and state agencies, as well as statutory laws. Congressional or legislative laws are enacted with the intention of protecting the public from professional malpractice, fraud, and financial impropriety, and to ensure public health and safety. It directly impacts businesses or provider relationships in health care, or to provide healthcare for defined groups of people such as the chronically ill, disabled, elderly, mentally ill or impoverished. Insurance laws, while not intended to directly affect health care, influence the business and delivery of healthcare.

The Social Security Act and its Amendments are the federal legislation that established the Medicare and Medicaid healthcare programs. While the Medicare program is fully administered and funded by the federal government and employee contributions, the Medicaid programs are administered by the states and share the responsibility of financing the programs with the federal government. Many states have several Medicaid programs, some that overlap. Also see the Social Security Act Amendments of 1983 and the Medicare Modernization Act of 2003 (MMA), as well as their subsequent amendments. Some health lawyers focus their practice solely on disability law, compliance, fraud and abuse or Medicare and Medicaid matters.

The Centers for Medicare and Medicaid Services (CMS) implements regulations called Conditions of Participation (CoPs) and provides benefit policy manuals inclusive of *Conditions of Coverage (CfC)* that health care organizations or practitioners must meet in order to participate in the Medicare and Medicaid programs and to be reimbursed for services rendered, respectively. The regulations (CoPs) focus primarily on the health and safety of the patients/residents and serve as the foundation for protecting beneficiaries and improving quality. Examples of the application of CoPs and CfCs include, but are not limited to, hospitals, skilled nursing facilities, home health agencies, hospices, and ambulatory surgical centers. See: *https://www.cms.gov/Regulations-andGuidance/Legislation/CFCAndCops.*

ADMINISTRATIVE LAW AND REGULATION

Administrative agencies are designed to function as agents of the executive branch of the government, protecting the public interest. A strong working knowledge of administrative law is essential for a health care law practice. The United States Department of Health and Human Services (HHS) is the Federal agency that oversees the Centers for Medicare and Medicaid Services (CMS). This government agency oversees and regulates the compliance of Medicare and Medicaid programs, thereby ensuring coverage and payment for these services. The United States Department of Veterans Affairs (DVA) is a peer agency to HHS and provides health care services for veterans. However, VA regulations and payment requirements may differ from Medicare requirements. The Office for Civil Rights (OCR) also contributes to compliance oversight and is responsible for protecting individuals' civil rights regarding to health care.

Each state has its own Department of Health (DOH) and Department of Human Services (DHS), under which they implement and manage the state Medicaid and other health care programs. Further, CMS usually contracts with the state Department of Health to survey and enforce the Medicare and Medicaid Conditions of Participation (CoPs).

The states also have the authority to regulate the practice of healthcare practitioners through State Licensing Boards, which are vested with broad powers to implement regulations through statutory practice acts. Many nurse attorneys have professional defense practices representing providers before their state boards, such as the Board of Medicine or the Board of Nursing.

Administrative law has its courts and judges. Agencies have the authority to impose substantial fines, demand repayment, require mandatory oversight, implement corrective actions, and, worst of all, exclude practitioners from participating in any entity that accepts federal funds. Keep in mind that almost every hospital and provider receives some Medicare and or Medicaid payments for services. Once a provider is excluded, they can no longer work in any capacity, even as a floor unit secretary. Health care lawyers can play an important role in avoiding or modifying these rulings.

TORT LAW

The most familiar basis for individual liability of nurses, physicians, and other health care providers, including hospitals, is tort law. This is often referred to aş medical negligence or medical malpractice stemming from the duty of care. Tort law has shaped and defined many health care quality and safety standards.

CONTRACT LAW

Contract law is a prominent mechanism that facilitates health care services and transactions. The complex network of healthcare contracts extends but is not limited to health care contracts between insurance companies and consumers, as well as agreements between insurance carriers and provider hospitals, physicians in private practice, employment contract drafting and negotiating, durable medical equipment companies, pharmacies, accountable care organizations, electronic medical records, practice management companies, and others. Competent contracting negotiations and legal scrutiny are crucial for successful healthcare business transactions, including the buying and selling of healthcare businesses and other business relationships between healthcare entities and third-party businesses. Nurse attorneys have the advantage of being aware of what is customary and standard for employers and third-party entities to include in health care contracts, such as the reasonable professional duties an employee can expect to perform.

Additionally, contracts govern the relationships between the Centers for Medicare & Medicaid Services (CMS) and the State Survey Agency's agreement to monitor certified Medicare healthcare providers in that State. Also, CMS contracts with companies to pay and audit Medicare claims, ensuring compliance with the Medicare program's requirements and billing standards. These are called Medicare Administrative Contractors (MACs). Other examples of healthcare government contractors are Recovery Auditor Contractors (RACs), Quality Improvement Organizations (QICs), Zone Program Integrity Contractors (ZPICs), and United Program Integrity Contractors (UPICs).

CORPORATE LAW

Corporate law is often utilized for provider entity matters, incorporations, employee and employer matters, incorporating new practices, general counsel positions for inpatient and outpatient settings, buying and selling practices, or entities. This practice requires knowledge of both applicable federal and state laws, as well as compliance with those federal, state, and local laws, as well as professional codes. Drafting, reviewing, and negotiating contracts is often a significant part of a corporate health law practice.

TRANSACTIONAL LAW PRACTICE

Corporate law and contract law are often considered transactional law matters. Transactional law is different from litigation or professional defense practices. Transactional law allows an attorney licensed in one state to represent a client in another state as long as the attorney is working on a matter governed by federal law. You do not go to the other state for any reason, including filing or appearing before a court without proper steps taken, meeting with a client, or representing the client in a hearing. Many aspects of health care contracts and corporate matters are governed by federal law, as well as state law.

CRIMINAL LAW

Under health care laws, criminal fines, penalties, or imprisonment may be levied, including felonies associated with Medicare, Medicaid, or other government insurance reimbursement fraud, unlawful billing practices, prohibited referral activities, or misrepresentation of practitioner qualifications. Each of the following Acts can result in steep monetary penalties, exclusion from federal health care programs, and possible imprisonment.

- In particular, the federal **Anti-Kickback Statute** (AKS) is a criminal statute that prohibits the exchange, or an offer to exchange, anything of value in an effort to induce referrals to federal or state health care programs. Each state may also have its own anti-kickback statute. The AKS is an anti-corruption statute intended to guard against overutilization, increased costs, and poor-quality services by prohibiting the influence of money, the gift of things of value, or the promise of referral business. Convictions, fines, and penalties for each violation can range from $25,000 to $100,000 and may include up to ten years of imprisonment.
- The **Stark regulations** are complex and wide-reaching, applying to physicians, as well as their ownership (or family ownership) of health care entities to which they refer business directly or indirectly. A Stark analysis needs to be considered in most contract and corporate matters. Many states have enacted their own versions of the Stark regulations, which can include other prohibited referrals or business relationships, as well as other health care professionals. Stark has safe harbors that allow, under very specific circumstances, legal arrangements that the general Stark regulations would

otherwise prohibit. For example, there is a safe harbor that allows a hospital in a medically underserved or rural area to recruit and financially support a new physician into that area. There is also a Stark compensation formula that applies to determining allowable physician compensation. This is an example of how federal law applies to physician contracts in every state.

- The **False Claims Act** is another complex and far-reaching Statute that has been applied not only to Medicare and Medicaid but also to commercial insurance claims and to the requirements for documentation in medical records to support claims filed for payment. The Act generally interpret it as a crime if a provider files a claim that is considered false for payment by the government. Federal and State False Claims Acts prohibit the payment of claims (bills) for services that do not meet Medicare or Medicaid coverage requirements. Some States have criminal statutes that encourage the prosecution of healthcare workers in cases of intentional or neglectful patient care, billing fraud, or prohibited financial arrangements stemming from this Act. Recently, the False Claims Act has been applied to non-health care billing and funding matters.

ESTABLISHING AND MAINTAINING A CLIENT BASE

Solo practitioners of healthcare law may have worked in large law firms. They may already have a book of business representing hospitals, nursing facilities, or home health care and hospice agencies, to name a few types of providers. Some attorneys have worked outside the hospital or clinical practice health care setting during their clinical practice years. They have established contacts with providers, professional leaders, and medical and professional associations that can serve as a valuable client base to support the growth of a solo practice. Some were specialized nurses or focused their law studies on specific areas of health care law. This provides the attorney with the clinical and legal knowledge necessary for a health law practice.

We highly recommend that the health care attorney join professional organizations such as The American Association of Nurse Attorneys (TAANA), the American Health Law Association (AHLA) and or the American Bar Association (ABA) Health Law Section as well as the practitioner's State Bar health law section to keep abreast of current State and federal issues and to develop collaborative relationships with like-minded practitioners. Several excellent email listservs can help solo practitioners to stay informed on the constantly changing health care laws. CMS and the Office of Civil Rights (OCR) send regular updates on compliance and specific changes that apply to your clients. We also recommend attending CLE programs to enhance your understanding and application of new or developing laws, agency rulings, and case law. The Health Care Compliance Association (HCCA) offers membership and certifications in health care compliance and health care privacy compliance, providing robust opportunities throughout the year to network and learn from other compliance professionals. Most hospitals have a Risk Manager. This position is often held by a nurse attorney who understands both legal and health care requirements.

Additionally, to grow your practice, we recommend that you join the State or national association(s) for the provider entities you, as a solo practitioner, wish to represent. You may wish to volunteer to speak at professional conferences, attend professional association meetings, or contribute to newsletters as a way to network and meet potential new clients. These memberships and participation in association activities will provide a means to stay updated in the field and to meet and collaborate with others. Such examples of national associations include the American Hospital Association (AHA), The American Health Care Association/National

Center for Assisted Living (AHCA/NCAL) for long term care nursing facilities and assisted living, the National Association of Home Care & Hospice (NAHC), the National Association of Hospice and Palliative Care (NHPCO) and State medical and nursing associations and boards. If you have an interest in a specific disease or a client in a particular situation, such as the American Cancer Society or AARP, you can also contact them to offer to be an organizational resource, legal advisor, or client referral source.

KEY STATUTES AND REGULATIONS

Examples of key statutes and regulations applicable to the Health Care Law Practice (not all inclusive):

Social Security Act Amendments of 1965 and 1983 (Medicare and Medicaid Health Insurance Programs)

- ***Medicare Modernization Act of 2003 (Medicare Part C and Part D programs)***
- ***Emergency Medical Treatment and Active Labor Act of 1986 (EMTALA)***
  - Includes the Consolidated Omnibus Budget Reconciliation Act (COBRA) of 1986 to give employees an option to continue their employer health insurance coverage by personal payment for a period of time, modified in 2025
- ***Health Insurance Portability and Accountability Act (HIPAA)***
- ***Health Information Technology for Economic and Clinical Health Act (HITECH)***
  - This Act was enacted as part of the American Recovery and Reinvestment Act (ARRA) of 2009 to regulate electronic records and data utilized in health care. It was expanded in 2025 to govern electronic health care communications and security, with the introduction of the Electronic Security Rules,

in response to the overwhelming expansion of hacking and ransomware attacks on health care entities' data.

- ***Patient Protection and Affordable Care Act (Also known as the Affordable Care Act, the ACA or "Obamacare") (includes the Elder Justice Act)***

- ***Federal False Claims Act (also consider State False Claims Acts) (False Claims Act was enacted after the Civil War, and more recently applied to health care billing matters)***
- ***The Federal Anti-Kickback Statute and Safe Harbor exceptions (also consider State and Federal Anti-Kickback laws)***
- ***Stark Regulations and Safe Harbor exceptions (prohibited referrals for physicians)(also referred to as "Stark")***
- ***Medicare and Medicaid regulations***
- ***The Americans with Disabilities Act (ADA)***
- ***The Family Medical Leave Act (FMLA) (also see State versions and related sick leave acts)***
- ***The Children's Health Insurance Program (CHIP)***
- ***Social Security Disability Insurance (SSDI)***
- ***Patient Safety and Quality Improvement Act***
- ***State: medical records laws, provider practice acts, privacy laws, health occupations laws, professional corporation laws***

AT THE TIME OF THIS BOOK'S PUBLICATION, 2025, MANY HEALTH CARE AGENCIES, FEDERAL AND STATE LAWS ARE IN TRANSITION. REFERENCES IN THIS SECTION NEED TO BE RESEARCHED AND CONFIRMED AT THE TIME OF USE.

***

LITIGATION PRACTICE

Kathleen A. McCormac, BSN, JD

DISCLOSURE

THE AUTHOR HAS NO FINANCIAL INTERESTS OR RELATIONSHIPS WITH ANY OF THE PRODUCTS OR PROGRAMS SUGGESTED IN THIS CHAPTER, NOR DO THEY ENDORSE THEM.

DISCLAIMER

WHILE THIS CHAPTER GUIDEBOOK OFFERS GUIDANCE ON SOLO PRACTICE, IT SHOULD NOT BE CONSTRUED AS LEGAL ADVICE.

Working with clients in litigation matters is interesting and challenging work for solo practitioners. Most claims involve underlying issues requiring expertise and experience to manage a claim safely. Litigators handle civil lawsuits before, during, and after trial.

OVERVIEW OF LITIGATION CLAIMS

Nurse attorneys in litigation have a wide range of areas of practice. Many represent parties in medical malpractice cases, while others represent them in civil or contract matters. The solo practitioner needs to assess what type of assistance, both human and technological, they need to successfully represent clients in litigation claims. Tasks vary based on the dispute, the attorney's experience, and the party being represented.

Most solo practitioners have experience in a larger firm where they learned the necessary components for representing clients. Here is a partial list:

- Intake system
- Conflict check system
- Calendaring system
- Case filing software
- Written discovery

- Subpoenas
- Deposition expertise
- Trial and/or arbitration experience

PHASES

INVESTIGATION AND ASSESSMENT

Litigation attorneys for the plaintiff conduct initial case investigations to determine if the evidence is adequate to file a lawsuit. Defense counsel will assess the evidence for claims brought against their clients. Many attorneys engage in pre-litigation efforts to settle cases.

PLEADINGS

Counsel for Plaintiffs and Defendants file a number of pleadings and motions in Court connected to litigation. Plaintiff's counsel initiates the case with the complaint and summons, and defense counsel responds with an answer and or counterclaim.

Counsel may draft a number of motions prior to a trial to limit or dismiss the case. There may be motions related to the venue where the case is set and other discovery-related motions.

DISCOVERY

During the discovery process, relevant information is exchanged in writing through interrogatories that the opposing party must answer. Depositions are taken for oral testimony under oath to further understand the facts of the matter. Documents relevant to the matter may be subpoenaed. Experts may need to be retained to analyze the facts based on the discovery.

PRE-TRIAL WORK

The time immediately before a trial usually involves expert depositions, pre-trial conferences, and motions to determine the scope of the evidence and witnesses. Counsel will develop a trial strategy to set their client's case in the best light.

TRIAL

Trial is an around-the-clock process for most cases, with the days spent in court presenting the matter and the time after court spent preparing for the next day. The development of the case may change based on the evidence presented. Jury selection is done with a voir dire process, assuming the matter is not a bench trial. Many attorneys hire jury consultants to help them select the best jurors for their client's case. Next, opening statements are given, followed by the presentation of evidence through witnesses and documents. Closing statements or summations are then given by counsel to the jury. The jury then deliberates and renders its verdict.

POST-TRIAL

There are a number of considerations post-verdict. There may be motions to set aside the verdict, opportunities to settle the matter, or an appeal of the verdict that litigation counsel may or may not want to or be qualified to handle.

CHAPTER 9

SELF-CARE

Barbara Forshier, RN, BSN, JD

DISCLOSURE

THE AUTHOR HAS NO FINANCIAL INTERESTS OR RELATIONSHIPS WITH ANY OF THE PRODUCTS OR PROGRAMS SUGGESTED IN THIS CHAPTER, NOR DO THEY ENDORSE THEM.

DISCLAIMER

WHILE THIS CHAPTER GUIDEBOOK OFFERS GUIDANCE ON SOLO PRACTICE, IT SHOULD NOT BE CONSTRUED AS LEGAL ADVICE.

Lawyers have consistently been a profession with a high rate of substance use disorder, depression, and even suicide. Most state bar associations have Lawyer Assistance Programs that offer help free of charge. Attorneys must take care of themselves first, just like the flight attendant who says to put on your own oxygen mask before helping others. Attorneys must also prioritize self-care to advocate for their clients properly.

Working as a solo or small firm attorney certainly has its benefits. However, it also has drawbacks. If you are a solo/small practitioner, you may not have support staff. You may be the paralegal, the receptionist, and the office administrator. Making time for self-care can seem self-defeating.

TIPS FOR SELF-CARE

DIET

Eat a healthy, well-balanced diet. Avoid excess sugar and caffeine, which will produce highs and lows in your energy levels throughout the day. Instead, have healthy snacks available when you feel a craving to munch. Vegetable sticks, string cheese, grapes, and other fruits provide a healthy alternative to sweets. Use hot, non-caffeinated tea as an alternative to coffee and always have a water bottle on your desk.

DAILY EXERCISE

This can be as little as walking for 10–20 minutes at lunchtime (which will make you take a break). Keep small dumbbells under your desk to exercise your arms while you are on a hand-free phone call. Join a gym (and go there to exercise), find walking buddies, or walk the dog. Just move.

TIME MANAGEMENT

Schedule time away from your desk. Use practice management software, organize your area, and don't procrastinate (like I did for this chapter). Set times to answer emails and phone calls. Set boundaries for yourself. Most of us do not need to be available to the client 24/7. Be protective of your time to do what is important to you.

HUMOR

Laugh. It releases endorphins, those little things in your body that energize you and make you feel good. Find a favorite show or call a funny friend. And remember it's okay to laugh at yourself.

DON'T TAKE IT PERSONALLY

If a case doesn't go your way, know that you did not put your client in their position. You have done the best you could with the cards dealt. Be picky when you can. If there are red flags on the initial interview, don't take the case.

PRAYER/MEDITATION/MINDFULNESS

- Prayer: We all need the help of a higher power at times, and it is okay to ask for that help.
- Meditation is a complementary therapy that you can do anytime and anywhere. It is a way to clear your mind and produce relaxation. It takes practice to learn the technique, and many sites are available to help you. Start with as little as 1 minute and work up to the desired length of time.
- Mindfulness: Is the practice of being present, being aware of where you are and what you are doing and trying not to be overly reactive or overwhelmed by what is happening around you.
- Breathing: Focused, periodic, deep, and relaxing breathing. One technique is the 4-7-8 breathing, or relaxing breath, which helps you concentrate on deep breaths. The practice is simple: Breathe in for a count of 4, hold for a count of 7, and breathe out for a count of 8. Practicing this for four breaths daily or more can help relieve anxiety and stress.

MUSIC

Listening to relaxing background music can help reduce stress. Music has been studied in healthcare and shown to decrease stress and anxiety. *Pandora* is a free app for Android through Google Play (if you don't mind commercials). Pandora lets you choose whatever type of music gets you through your day.

AROMATHERAPY

This is another therapy utilized in healthcare and can be used daily in your practice. Use candles or aromatherapy diffusers with your favorite essential oil, depending on your needs. Lavender is known for its calming effect.

MASSAGE

We all know how we feel after being in front of the computer all day. Schedule a massage to help with those tight muscles. Take this time for you.

SLEEP

Yes, we all need it. First, you must manage your time. Establish a routine, read a book, turn off your electronics, and let your body slow down. Use meditation if you have difficulty turning off your mind. The National Sleep Foundation advises that adults should get between seven and nine hours of sleep each night. Sleep is a basic need, so do not short yourself here. If you find that you are sleepy throughout the day or you have been told you snore loudly or stop breathing, seek medical assistance. You may be advised to do a sleep study to improve your sleep effectiveness. You can often do such a study at home.

FIND YOUR TRIBE

I found my tribe with TAANA. This is your group of like-minded individuals, where you feel you belong. Create your own community TAANA tribe. Being a solo or small attorney means you can't just walk down the hall to seek advice or bounce ideas off a colleague. In my area, we started a TAANA nurse license defense group. We meet quarterly for breakfast to discuss issues and strategies to serve our clients better. We also have a legislative agenda and work with the state nurses' union to move our mutual agendas for the benefit of nurses.

With the social isolation prevalent in a solo/small practice, seek other groups through your bar association, too. There are solo/small groups in most bar associations, women's attorney associations, defense attorney associations, etc.

VOLUNTEER

Give back, whether by providing legal services or volunteering at your local animal shelter to walk the dogs. It feels good and also relieves the stress we encounter in our own narrow confines.

Your wellness matters. Take care of yourself, recognize the signs of stress and anxiety, and never be afraid to ask for help.

Thank You for Reading *Solo Practice Guidebook*

We hope this guidebook has helped you develop a blueprint for your own journey on the challenging and rewarding path of solo law practice. Jurisdictional requirements vary considerably; therefore, we did not intend this guidebook to provide legal advice.

Our goals are to outline the steps needed to set up a successful solo practice and identify resource suggestions for moving in the right direction.

You can access additional valuable collegial resources at The American Association of Nurse Attorneys (TAANA). To learn more about TAANA's opportunities for nurse attorneys and others interested in legal issues as they relate to the health care industry, visit https://www.taana.org.

A quote attributed to Seneca sums up our good luck wish for you.

Luck is what happens when preparation meets opportunity.

Seneca

Contributors and Reviewers

Although academic convention lists degrees before licenses, we have chosen to place our nursing credentials first.

Adrienne R. Abner, RN, JD, LLM, MBA, MSN, NE-BC, is a Pennsylvania attorney, currently practicing as a staff attorney with the Pennsylvania Institutional Law Project, doing civil litigation and advocacy to increase access to medication for opioid use disorders (MOUD) and medication-assisted treatment (MAT) for incarcerated people. Adrienne has interned with the Rhode Island Public Defenders as an appellate clerk, student attorney, and with Chisholm, Chisholm & Kilpatrick LTD, Veterans Appeal Firm in Rhode Island. Before beginning a second career in law, Adrienne had a progressive career in nursing and health care administration, including positions as an Assistant Vice-President Nursing, and Vice-President of Patient Services at Community Hospital – Crozer-Keystone Health System in Pennsylvania, Area Vice-President Northeast Operations for Healogics, Inc., in Florida, and Director of Outpatient Wound Care and Hyperbaric Oxygen Medicine with Christiana Health Care System in Delaware. Adrienne is also a Board-certified Nurse Executive with the American Nurses Credentialing Center.

Adrienne holds a Juris Doctor degree from Roger Williams University School of Law, a Master of Laws degree in Health Law and Policy from Hofstra University School of Law, a Master of Science degree in Nursing, Clinical Specialist from the University of Pennsylvania, a Bachelor of Science degree in Nursing from Widener University and a Master of

Business Administration degree from Wilmington University. Adrienne is the proud recipient of the Roger Williams University Class of 2018 Barristers' Award. In addition to her TAANA membership, she is a proud member of the Sigma Theta Tau International Eta Beta Chapter (Past-President), Phi Alpha Delta Law Fraternity International Kennedy Chapter, and Alpha Kappa Alpha Sorority, Incorporated Sigma Zeta Omega Chapter.

Melanie Balestra, RN, PNP, MN, JD, is a transactional and administrative law attorney as well as an active Pediatric Nurse Practitioner at the Laguna Beach Community Clinic. She is the owner and Senior Attorney at the Law Offices of Melanie Balestra, Irvine, California. Ms. Balestra has practiced as a nurse practitioner for over thirty years and as an attorney for over twenty years. She has been on the faculty of Montana State University, University of South Florida, Washington State University, California State University, Los Angeles and continues as an Adjunct Lecturer at the University of California, Irvine, and UCLA.

Ms. Balestra focuses on liability, disciplinary and business issues that affect physicians, physician assistants, nurses, nurse practitioners, and other health care providers, as well as hospitals and health insurance. She addresses and solves compliance issues for various hospital facilities and group practices. She has written multiple journal articles and lectured nationally on liability issues for nurses and nurse practitioners. She provides expert witness testimony for both healthcare boards and professionals.

Ms. Balestra is counsel for the California Association of Nurse Practitioners and on the Advisory Board of Nurses Service Organization. She is a past President of the California Coalition for Nurse Practitioners, the American College of Nurse Practitioners and The American Association of Nurse Practitioners, and was the 2017 president of TAANA. She is licensed to practice before California and Arizona courts as well as the US Supreme Court. She is a volunteer advocate for patients and does pro bono work for patients as well as volunteering abroad as a nurse practitioner in Africa, Cambodia, and Mexico. She is involved in advocacy for mental health and has published a best-selling book on Amazon, *Suicide: A Mother's Journey Through Her Child's Pain.*

Edie Brous RN, BSN, MS, MPH, JD, is a nurse attorney in private practice, concentrating on professional licensure representation, medical malpractice defense, and nursing advocacy. She has practiced in major litigation law firms representing nurses, physicians, hospitals, and pharmaceutical companies. Edie is admitted to practice before the Bars of the State Courts of New York, New Jersey, and Pennsylvania**,** the Southern and Eastern Districts of the New York Federal Courts and the United States Supreme Court. She is a member of many bar associations and nursing organizations and was the 2011 president of TAANA.

Ms. Brous has an extensive clinical and managerial background in OR, Emergency and Critical Care Nursing. In addition to her law degree, she holds Master's Degrees in Public Health and in Critical Care Nursing from Columbia University. She has been part-time faculty at Columbia University and has held adjunct faculty positions at several universities, teaching legal aspects of nursing. Ms. Brous has lectured and published extensively on legal issues for nurses and co-authored the textbook *Law and Ethics for Advanced Practice Nurses.* She is the 2008 recipient of the Outstanding Advocate Award, the 2017 Outstanding Litigation Member Award, and the 2020 Outstanding Solo Practice Section Member Award from The American Association of Nurse Attorneys.

Adam D. Brown, RN, JD, is a practicing attorney in Dahlonega, Georgia, initially as a sole practitioner and now at Brown & Adams, LLC. He has been nominated to Super Lawyers, Georgia's Defense of Drinking Drivers Institute, and the National College of DUI Defense. Additionally, while in nursing school, he served as the President of the Tennessee Association of Student Nurses.

Lorie A. Brown, RN, MN, JD, obtained her law degree from Indiana University, Indianapolis, Indiana, in 1990. Lorie founded Brown Law Office, P.C. in 1999 and began working as a legal nurse consultant and representing nurses and other healthcare providers before the licensing boards. She also mentors nurses on how to start their own business. Lorie has authored three books: *Law and Order for Nurses: The Easy Way to Protect Your License and Your Livelihood*, *From Frustrated to Fulfilled: The Empowered Nurses System*, and *The Legal Nurse Consultant's Workbook: Turning Your Nursing Knowledge into a Successful Consulting Practice*. Lorie was the 2021 president of TAANA. She has a weekly blog on either www.YourNurseAttorney.com or www.EmpoweredNurses.org. She has been a keynote speaker and speaker at many regional and national nursing organization conferences and is the author of numerous published articles.

Conswella M. Byrd, RN, BSN, JD, received a Bachelor of Arts degree in History from the University of Illinois, Chicago. She is a registered nurse, licensed to practice in California, with a Bachelor of Science in Nursing from the University of California, San Francisco. Her nursing specialty was neonatology. She received a JD from the University of California, Hastings College of the Law and is an attorney admitted to the State Bar of California, the US District Court Bar, the US Court of Appeals for the Ninth Circuit Bar and the US Supreme Court Bar.

Ms. Byrd's law practice focuses on estate planning, wills, trusts, and powers of attorney. She has an extensive background in higher education, having taught wills and trusts as a law school and paralegal professor. She has also taught legal issues in nursing and healthcare as a nursing school and health sciences professor at California State University East Bay, and has published several articles on legal issues in *Nursing*.

Ms. Byrd was the Director, Paralegal and Legal Nurse Consultant Programs, at California State University East Bay. She is a former President of the Northern California Chapter of TAANA. In 1993, she received the TAANA Outstanding Chapter Member award for her development of the Legal Nurse Consultant Section.

Flynn Carey, JD, focuses his practice on the defense of licensed professionals, criminal defense, school discipline, and Title IX litigation. Mr. Carey is one of only three attorneys recognized by the State Bar of Arizona as a certified specialist in administrative law. He represents licensed and certificated professionals before their licensing boards and agencies when facing possible discipline or allegations of unprofessional conduct, and in conjunction with parallel criminal allegations. Mr. Carey appears on behalf of clients before the majority of licensing, regulatory, and professional boards in Arizona.

Kim M. Crump, RN, BS, BA, JD, started her legal career before her nursing career. She attended the North Carolina Central University School of Law, serving as Law Review Note Editor. After attaining her law degree, she served as a commissioned officer in the Navy Judge Advocate General's Corps, receiving the Navy Achievement Medal in 1987. After serving seven years in the Navy, she pursued a private practice in Norfolk, VA, focusing on criminal defense, domestic relations, and personal injury.

While practicing law, Ms. Crump returned to school and obtained her nursing degree from Old Dominion University. She then worked as an emergency room nurse at the Children's Hospital of The King's Daughters. She was featured in a *The Virginian-Pilot* article entitled "Lawyer by Day…nurse by night" because while she practiced nursing at night, she continued her law practice during the day. In addition to her law and nursing degrees, she also obtained a Bachelor's Degree in Psychology from the University of Virginia. She loves utilizing her nursing and psychology knowledge in her law practice, finding them both very useful.

Ms. Crump, in addition to her private practice, currently sits part-time as a Substitute Judge in General District and Juvenile Domestic Relations District courts in the 3rd District of Virginia. She also serves as a Special Justice hearing commitment hearings in Portsmouth General District Court. Ms. Crump has her certification and serves as a guardian ad litem in the juvenile courts. She is and has been a member of many professional organizations, including the American Bar Association, the Old Dominion Bar Association, the South Hampton Roads Bar Association, TAANA, the Federal Bar Association and Alpha Kappa Alpha Sorority, Inc.

Robert Esgro, R.Ph., Esq. is a practicing pharmacist and attorney specializing in health law, including OIG and regulatory compliance, FDA consulting, drug diversion, lease review, policy and procedure drafting, and civil litigation support. He has spoken at national meetings on various topics of health law.

Barbara A. Forshier, RN, BSN, JD, is a nurse attorney who has been an advocate for nurses throughout her 40-year nursing career. As a nurse, she was a union advocate and helped negotiate four union contracts. She returned to Law School to further enhance her advocacy skills. She currently owns and operates Forshier Law, LLC, representing licensed health care professionals, mostly nurses, before their respective Boards.

Barbara obtained her law degree while working as a nurse and attending law school on weekends at Hamline University School of Law in St. Paul. She subsequently became a law clerk for a Ramsey County judge before opening her own practice in 2010. She has been a staunch advocate for safe nurse staffing levels and was elected to the Minnesota Nurses Association ("MNA") Governmental Affairs Commission for two terms.

Additionally, she served as union chairperson in her 1,200-nurse hospital, where she represented nurses in disciplinary hearings, participated on nursing practice and labor-management committees and encouraged nurses to stay strong during a seven-week nursing strike in 2016.

Her area of nursing specialty was perianesthesia nursing, where she was certified in both ambulatory perianesthesia nursing (CAPA) and post-anesthesia nursing (CPAN). She also co-authored a research paper titled "Adult Perianesthesia Do Not Resuscitate Orders: A Systematic Review," which was published in the *Journal of Perianesthesia Nursing*, June 20, 2019.

Paula DiMeo Grant, RN, BSN, MA, JD, is a nurse attorney admitted to practice law in the District of Columbia. Her experience includes litigation, mediation and nursing disciplinary defense. From 1991 to 2012, she served as a mediator for the Superior Court of the District of Columbia. From 1998 to 2004, she was Of Counsel to Ross & Hardies, now McGuireWoods, LLP. She has held adjunct faculty positions, teaching nursing and law courses, and has also published on the subject. Ms. Grant is the recipient of the Cynthia Northrop Distinguished Service Award and TAANA Board of Directors Award. She is also a former member of TAANA Board of Directors and a former president of TAANA Foundation. Ms. Grant is AV Preeminent rated by Martindale-Hubbell.

Karen J. Halpern, RN, BS, MSN, JD, was a litigation attorney in solo private practice with an office in Melville, New York (now retired). She is admitted to practice law in the New York State and Federal Courts. Her law practice for the past 32 years has been limited to medical malpractice defense litigation and professional licensure defense representing doctors, nurses and other health care professionals. She has lectured extensively on a variety of health law-related topics, including professional licensure defense and medical malpractice litigation. She has held adjunct faculty positions at SUNY Stony Brook, Adelphi University and Duquesne University, where she has taught courses in legal issues, ethics, and forensic nursing. Before becoming an attorney, she was a registered nurse with 12 years' experience as a labor and delivery room nurse. She holds a Bachelor of Science Degree in Nursing from SUNY Stony Brook, a Master of Science Degree in Forensic Nursing from Duquesne University and a Juris Doctor degree from Touro Law School.

Kathleen A. Hessler, RN, JD, CHC, CHPC, is Principal of Hessler Consulting, LLC. Until April 2020, she was the national Director of Compliance & Risk for Simione Healthcare Consultants, LLC, where she was responsible for a team of compliance professionals providing ethics, compliance and risk management services to home health and hospice companies and working with attorneys to defend the agencies in allegations of fraud and abuse. She served four years on the Board of Directors for the Texas and New Mexico Hospice Organization and chaired the Health Law and Compliance Section of TAANA.

Ms. Hessler is a frequent speaker at state and national healthcare and legal conferences and authored the chapter involving health care law in the third edition of the nursing textbook, *Concepts for Nursing Practice*, which was published in February 2020. Ms. Hessler practiced healthcare law for 17 years, representing long-term and post-acute care companies. From 2010–2012, Ms. Hessler served as Director of Risk Management for CHRISTUS St. Vincent Regional Medical Center in Santa Fe, NM, where she was a member of the hospital ethics committee. In addition to her degrees in law and nursing, she holds certificates in Health Care Ethics, Compliance, and HIPAA Privacy Compliance.

Diane J. Knoblauch, RN, MSN, JD, is licensed as a nurse and an attorney in Ohio and Michigan. She began her nursing career as a diploma nurse, obtained a BSN from Madonna University, and an MSN from Wayne State University with a major in primary care. She was certified as an adult nurse practitioner through the American Nurses Association and the American Academy of Nurse Practitioners. From 1981 to 1991, her clinical practice focused on primary care and occupational health. Her last clinical practice as a nurse practitioner in occupational health was in 1991 at the University of Michigan Medical Center. While attending law school, she was an assistant professor of nursing at Medical College of Ohio (now University of Toledo) in the undergraduate and graduate programs, participated in developing the Nurse Practitioner program and was one of the first two faculty in that program. She continued her clinical practice in the Surgical Intensive Care Unit at the University of Michigan, retiring in December 2018.

Ms. Knoblauch has practiced as an attorney since 1994. Her law practice focuses on estate planning, elder law, nursing and farming. She continues to provide lectures and seminars on legal and ethical issues in nursing. Ms. Knoblauch represents nurses before the Michigan and Ohio Boards of Nursing. She served as President of TAANA in 2022, TAANA Board of Directors from 2017–2023, TAANA Foundation from 2024–present, and is currently the treasurer.

Randi Kopf, RN, MS, JD, has had a corporate, regulatory and eHealth law practice, Kopf HealthLaw, LLC, www.KopfHealthlaw.com, since 1994. She is a nationally recognized and sought-after speaker for professional organizations on healthcare law, corporate matters, HIPAA, HITECH, EHR, HIT, professional and regulatory matters, including the ACA, Stark, Medicare, and health insurance. She provides health law counsel to physicians, allied health practitioners, medical groups, national and regional medical and allied health associations, locally and nationally.

Her credentials include University of Maryland School of Law, J.D., State University of New York at Stony Brook, School of Nursing, B.S., M.S., Cornell University, B.S., and formerly Board-certified Family Nurse Practitioner (30 years). She is admitted to practice law in Maryland and the United States Supreme Court.

Ms. Kopf serves as an invited member of the Maryland Attorney Grievance Commission and has served on the Maryland Health Care Commission EDI/HIPAA task force that developed nationally accepted privacy guideline tools. She has provided legal support for several US Congressional health care bills and advocated on behalf of physicians before the US Attorney's Health Care Fraud Task Force. Randi was Chair of the Montgomery County Bar Association Health Law Section.

She continues to hold leadership positions in the Bar and professional associations. She is currently the President of TAANA Foundation and President of Chesapeake Nurse Attorneys, Inc. She served as an Officer and Member of the TAANA Board of Directors, was a longtime editor and author for the *Journal of Nursing Law* and is currently a reviewer for the *Journal for Nurse Practitioners.* Randi served on the Board of Directors for the Charles E. Smith Life Communities, Rockville, MD.

Prior to attending law school, Ms. Kopf's professional experience included years of clinical practice as a family/oncology nurse practitioner, as well as extensive teaching experience that includes instructor and faculty positions at Georgetown, the University of Maryland, and Adelphi University.

Her various published work includes *Compliance Program Guide Before You Sign … Managed Care Contract Review for Health Care Providers* and *The Nursing Handbook of Physical Assessment.* She served as editor and contributor for the *Business and Legal Guidebook for Nurse Practitioners*, published by TAANA.

The American Bar Association published "Antitrust Enforcement: How Medical Practices Feel the Effects" in the *Health Lawyer Journal.* Ms. Kopf has served on the Board of Advisors and contributed to *Managed Care Contract Negotiator* and *Health Information Compliance Insider,* contributed to *Medicare Compliance Alert, Medical Economics, BNA E-Health Reporter* and multiple other professional publications.

Some of Ms. Kopf's honors include the Cornell University Alumni Award for Outstanding Volunteerism, the National Distinguished Service Award in Nursing, being voted as a "Super Lawyer" for Maryland and DC, America's Most Honored Professional award (2014), and named Best Health Law Firm in Maryland by Legal Elite (2016). TAANA awarded her the Outstanding Legislative & Compliance Section Member Award (2017), Outstanding Advocate Award (2015), Cynthia Northrop Distinguished Service Award (2004 & 2011).

Rosemary Conlon McCarthy, RN, BSN, MS, JD, is a nurse attorney admitted to practice law in the State of Texas and the Supreme Court of the United States. She holds active licenses to practice nursing in New York and Texas. Her experience includes plaintiff medical malpractice and product liability, in-house counsel managing chemical tort litigation and general insurance defense. Throughout most of her nursing and legal careers, she has held various academic positions, the last being Associate Professor at Houston Baptist University, teaching healthcare law, ethics, and health policy content to graduate and undergraduate students in the College of Nursing and Master of Healthcare Administration Program.

Ms. McCarthy is a Founding Member of TAANA-TX, Past President of TAANA-TX, Past President of TAANA and a Trustee of TAANA Foundation. She is the recipient of TAANA's Cynthia Northrop Distinguished Service Award and the TAANA Board of Directors Award.

Humbly, she is the first recipient of the TAANA Lifetime Achievement and Appreciation Award.

Kathleen A. McCormac, BSN, JD, is a Nurse Attorney who practices in San Francisco. She graduated from the University of Missouri with a BSN and worked for 13 years as a pediatric nurse in a variety of settings throughout the country. Ms. McCormac graduated from Loyola Law School in 1991. She has represented employees in employment disputes since 1995. Kathy has litigated over 1,000 claims and has successfully arbitrated and tried cases for her clients. She has argued appellate cases related to disability discrimination before the California and 9th Circuit Courts. In addition, she represents health care workers in discipline matters before the California Professional Boards. Ms. McCormac is the Past President of TAANA and San Francisco Inns of Court. Ms. McCormac is a speaker and published author in her areas of expertise.

Janet E. Michael, BSN, MSN, JD, is a nurse attorney with a tri-state practice in Maine, Massachusetts, and New Hampshire. Ms. Michael's practice over the years has had a special focus on medical and nursing malpractice, professional practice issues (especially nursing standards of practice), disciplinary defense, and health-care risk management. She frequently represents nurses, nurse practitioners, mental health providers, and other allied health-care professionals before their professional Boards in Maine, New Hampshire, and Massachusetts.

Ms. Michael has written numerous articles for professional journals and spoken at many seminars and conferences on topics that relate to current and emerging legal, practice, ethical and risk management issues in health care.

Ms. Michael has a varied health care background, including work as a community health nurse, a nursing educator, a hospital charge nurse, a healthcare/risk management consultant, a medical malpractice specialist, and a nurse attorney. She is an active member of TAANA as well as a number of other professional associations, including the New Hampshire Bar Association, the Maine State Bar Association, and the Maine Trial Lawyers Association. TAANA awarded Ms. Michael the 2007 Outstanding Advocate Award. She received her B.S. in Nursing from the University of Maine Portland-Gorham, an M.S. in Community Health Nursing from Boston University, and a J.D. from Northeastern University.

Kathleen Russell, RN, MN, JD

Kathleen Russell, a lawyer and a nurse, was an Associate Director in the Division of Nursing Regulation for the National Council of State Boards of Nursing (NCSBN) (now retired). Kathleen's professional background includes 40 years of nursing, legal, and non-profit leadership experience. She practiced nursing as a pediatric clinical nurse specialist and nursing educator, and law as a trial attorney. At NCSBN, she is responsible for services provided to member boards, including investigation and discipline, National Practitioner Data Bank reporting, alternative to discipline programs, substance use disorder, licensure fraud, and, most recently, cannabis. She has written many professional articles and speaks on a variety of topics. She received a Power of Nursing Leadership Pinnacle Nurse Leader Award in 2020.

Teressa M. Sanzio, RN, MPA, JD, is a sole practitioner at The Law Office of Teressa M. Sanzio, P.C. in Phoenix, Arizona, where she devotes her practice to administrative and regulatory law. Teressa provides professional representation for all licensed health care providers with all licensure-related matters, including board complaints, application denials, and other matters. She has represented licensed professionals for over twenty years. Teressa also holds a master's degree in Public

Administration, a Bachelor of Science Degree in Business Administration, and an associate degree in Nursing. Teressa's nursing background is in ER and ICU. Prior to becoming an attorney, Teressa worked as a legal nurse consultant, a risk management consultant, and a nurse specialist in quality resource management.

Teressa was the 2015 President of TAANA, having served on the Board of Directors for approximately ten years. In 2015, Teressa received TAANA's Cynthia Northrop Distinguished Service Award. She is also the recipient of TAANA's Outstanding Advocate Award (2016) and Outstanding Education Award (2007). Teressa served on the Executive Council of the Administrative Law Section of the State Bar of Arizona, holding leadership roles from 2003 to 2009, including President. Teressa is currently serving on the Arizona State Bar Administrative Law Advisory Commission and the Examination Subcommittee for the Arizona Board of Legal Specialization in Administrative Law.

Teressa speaks locally and nationally on disciplinary defense of nurses. Teressa also proactively worked with the Arizona State Legislature in making new laws and amending existing statutes that benefit licensed health care professionals. Teressa is admitted to practice in all Arizona State Courts and in the United States Supreme Court.

Eileen M. Talamante, RN, BSN, JD, is a shareholder member of the law firm of Goodman Allen Donnelly, in Richmond, Virginia, where she concentrates her practice in the representation of nurses, physicians, and other health care professionals in licensing and discipline matters. Eileen received a Bachelor of Science in Nursing from the University of Wisconsin in 1988 and earned a law degree with honors from the University of Tennessee College of Law while working as a critical care nurse.

She is passionate about advocating on behalf of fellow nurses and other health care providers both as a lawyer and as a registered nurse. In addition to licensure defense, her practice includes credentialing, peer review matters, third-party payor inquiries/proceedings, and risk management issues. She regularly presents to nurses, physicians, pharmacists, hospital risk managers, physicians, and medical practice managers.

Eileen has served as Executive Committee Member of the Lewis F. Powell Jr., American Inn of Court, Richmond Chapter, and as President from 2017 to 2019. She has served as a TAANA board member and as President-Elect in 2021.

Eileen was honored with two prestigious awards in recognition of her outstanding advocacy on behalf of nurses during 2020, *The Year of the Nurse*. She was awarded the 2020 Outstanding Advocate Award from TAANA as well as the Virginia Nurses Foundation's (VNF) "2020 Year of the Nurse Award."

Eileen published the article, "2020 is Designated as The Year of the Nurse... WOW, is it Ever...". The article expressed her belief that nurses will become stronger, more empowered, and more resilient when faced with the unprecedented challenges brought about by the pandemic, and outlined multiple ways for nurses to practice self-care and protect their license. Her article received high reviews and was picked up for publishing in May of 2020 in *both* of the primary medical/legal publications in Virginia: *Virginia Lawyers Weekly* and the *Virginia Medical Law Report.*

Cassandra "Cassie" McCrary Williams, RN, BSN, JD, LLM, CNOR, is a seasoned principal attorney at the Law Offices of Cassandra M. Williams LLC, concentrating in the areas of nurse license defense, worker's compensation, workplace discrimination and contract law. A multi-faceted communicator and negotiator, Cassie has over 16 years of experience in drafting and negotiating complex agreements. Cassie also reviews employment contracts for physicians, nurses, and other health care professionals. A former nurse educator at Emery Hospital in Atlanta,

Georgia, Cassie continues to educate new nurses on the importance of protecting their license through speaking at various hospitals and nursing schools.

Cassie defends registered nurses, nurse practitioners, CRNAs (nurse anesthetists) and vocational nurses or LPNs from Board of Nursing accusations where the nurse is accused of violating the Nurse Practice Act.

She is an ordained minister, speaker, and personal coach, a published author, and a fierce advocate for nurses and veterans. Cassie served as a board member of The American Association of Nurse Attorneys.

Cassie has a Bachelor of Science in Nursing from Howard University and was commissioned in the United States Army Nurse Corps in 1993, where she served at Walter Reed Army Medical Center for four years on active duty. She has a law degree from Western Michigan Thomas M. Cooley Law School. She received a Master of Law in Healthcare Law from Georgia State University College of Law in 2016. She is barred in three states: Georgia, Virginia, and Michigan.

Hahnah Williams, RN, BSN, JD, is an attorney and registered nurse who owns a law firm in Atlanta, Georgia: Hahnah Williams, Attorney at Law, P.C. Hahnah holds a Juris Doctor Degree from Mercer University School of Law and a Bachelor of Science in Nursing Degree from Clayton State University. As a registered nurse turned lawyer with over 20 years of combined experience, Hahnah brings a unique perspective to the representation of healthcare professionals. Hahnah's law practice focuses on the defense of nurses, nurse practitioners, physicians, and other healthcare professionals in all aspects of professional license matters, including license applications, Board complaints, employer investigations, allegations of professional misconduct, allegations of drug diversion or abuse, and professional malpractice cases.

Hahnah also represents healthcare professionals in criminal matters and business transaction matters. In addition, Hahnah has conducted several seminars and webinars on legal issues in healthcare. Hahnah is the author and creator of the "Ask a Nurse Attorney" column published by the Georgia Nurses Association. Hahnah is the 2020 recipient of the Outstanding Advocate Award from TAANA.

Made in the USA
Coppell, TX
25 October 2025

61789462R00098